SOURCE AND SUMMIT

Source and Summit

*Six Great Spiritual Guides Talk
about the Eucharist*

JOEL GIALLANZA, CSC

ST PAULS

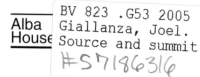
Library of Congress Cataloging-in-Publication Data

Giallanza, Joel.
  Source and summit : six great spiritual guides talk about the
Eucharist / by Joel Giallanza.
      p. cm.
  ISBN 0-8189-0979-X
  1. Lord's Supper—History of doctrines.   I. Title.

  BV823.G53 2005
  234'.163—dc22

                              2004028061

Produced and designed in the United States of America by the
Fathers and Brothers of the Society of St. Paul,
2187 Victory Boulevard, Staten Island, New York 10314-6603,
as part of their communications apostolate.

ISBN: 0-8189-0979-X

Printing Information:

Current Printing - first digit   1 2 3 4 5 6 7 8 9 10

Year of Current Printing - first year shown

2005 2006 2007 2008 2009 2010 2011 2012 2013 2014

DEDICATION

For my religious family,
the Brothers, Priests, and Sisters
of the Congregations of Holy Cross

TABLE OF CONTENTS

SOURCE AND SUMMIT

"This is My Body" — This is Our Way of Life

> While they were eating, he took a loaf
> of bread, and after blessing it he broke
> it, gave it to them, and said, "Take; this
> is my body." Then he took a cup, and
> after giving thanks he gave it to them,
> and all of them drank from it. He said
> to them, "This is my blood of the cov-
> enant, which is poured out for many."
> (Mark 14:22-24)

Simple actions of a host at table. Simple words to
inaugurate the greatest of gifts. A gift that will nourish
all those who walk in the footsteps of this host. Such
are the origins of the Eucharist, such are the origins of our life as Christians. This is nothing less
than Jesus' gift of himself for all who choose to live
his example, continue his mission, and preach his
message.

Since the time when those simple actions and
words were first accomplished, more than two mil-

lennia ago, the gift of the Eucharist has endured as the Church's greatest treasure. It has been an intriguing two thousand years to say the least. Over those centuries the Eucharist has been the subject of blessings and battles, of holiness and heresy, of dissertations and denunciations. Through it all, since that supper among friends in the Upper Room, the Eucharist has remained faithfully and powerfully present. This gift of Jesus himself remains with us even now.

"Source and Summit"

In speaking of our share in this gift, the Second Vatican Council teaches us that by "taking part in the eucharistic sacrifice, the source and summit of the Christian life, (we) offer the divine victim to God and (ourselves) along with it" (*Dogmatic Constitution on the Church*, 11). Source and Summit. The significance of this succinct description is twofold. First, it articulates the primary role of the Eucharist for the Christian community. The Church looks to the Eucharist to remember its origins and to have a glimpse of its destiny. As the People of God, we trace our Christian roots to the self-gift of Jesus in the Paschal Mystery. As we take part in this intimate sharing, among ourselves and with our Eucharistic Lord, we are challenged once again to remember and revitalize all that we are called to be by our common vocation, people of love and union.

Second, the Eucharist is also the source and summit of our individual lives as Christians, most especially of our identity as followers of Jesus. The very meaning of who and what we are is grounded in all that Jesus accomplished. His life, death, resurrection, and the gift of his continuing presence among us constitute the priorities by which we have been called to live. Those same priorities indicate the pathways of the spiritual journey toward what we are called to become. That journey engages us in nothing less than a transformation into the living likeness of the Lord Jesus. Truly, for us as community and as individuals, the Eucharist is the source and summit of our Christian life.

Six Great Saints, Teachers and Guides

There are many lenses through which the Eucharist can be viewed: Scripture, Church history, evolution of doctrine, magisterial teachings, and theological trends. For these present reflections we will view the Eucharist from the perspective of the spiritual life and the journey toward union with God on which Jesus leads and accompanies his followers.

Our teachers and guides for these reflections will be six great saints, three women and three men. In addition, each of these saints has been declared a Doctor of the Church; that is, the caliber of their teaching has spanned the centuries and has become part of the foundation upon which is built the Church's understanding of the spiritual life. The reflections offered here are designed to support us along the paths of our spiritual journey. Biographical, historical, and doctrinal material will be incorporated into each chapter insofar as it can assist us in understanding the message of that particular Doctor.

There are in the Church today thirty-three saints designated as Doctors of the Church. Three are women. The earliest Doctor, Saint Athanasius, lived in the fourth century; the latest Doctor, Saint Thérèse of Lisieux, lived during the latter part of the nineteenth century. Taken together, these thirty-three women and men represent a variety of cultures and theologies, and a diversity of countries and political regimes. The common threads among them, however, are their passionate love for Jesus and their determination to live his example and teaching to the best of their ability. Also, they were tireless in their efforts to encourage and lead others to live with that same passion and determination.

The six Doctors of the Church we will meet in these reflections were chosen not only for their consistent popularity and familiarity among many Christians, but especially because they have been and are wise teachers and guides for those who strive to probe and live the wisdom of the Church's rich mystical tradition. By way of introduction, only basic facts of life will be presented here; additional information is provided in each chapter. They are presented in chronological order.

Saint Catherine of Siena was born on March 25, 1347 at Siena, Italy and died on April 29, 1380. She was canonized in 1461 by Pope Pius II and declared a Doctor of the Church in 1970 by Pope Paul VI. Her feast day is April 29.

Saint Teresa of Avila was born on March 28, 1515 at Avila, Spain and died on October 4, 1582. She was canonized in 1622 by Pope Paul V and declared a Doctor of the Church in 1970 by Pope Paul VI, a few days before Saint Catherine of Siena. Her feast day is October 15.

Saint John of the Cross was born on June 24, 1542 at Fontiveros, Spain and died on December 14, 1591. He was canonized in 1726 by Pope Benedict XIII and declared a Doctor of the Church in 1926 by Pope Pius XI. His feast day is December 14.

Saint Francis de Sales was born on August 21, 1567 at Savoy, France and died on December 28, 1622. He was canonized in 1665 by Pope Alexander VII and declared a Doctor of the Church in 1877 by Pope Pius IX. His feast day is January 24.

Saint Alphonsus de Liguori was born on September 27, 1696 at Marianelli, Italy and died on August 1, 1787. He was canonized in 1839 by Pope Gregory XVI and declared a Doctor of the Church in 1871 by Pope Pius IX. His feast day is August 1.

Saint Thérèse of Lisieux was born on January 2, 1873 at Alençon, France and died on September 30, 1897. She was canonized in 1925 by Pope Pius XI and declared a Doctor of the Church in 1997 by Pope John Paul II. Her feast day is October 1.

In the book of Daniel we read, "Those who are wise shall shine like the brightness of the sky, and those who lead many to righteousness, like the stars forever and ever" (12:3). These words apply very well to the six great saints who will guide us through these reflections on the Eucharist. May we learn from their wisdom and their example, so our own daily life and work will reflect that Jesus alone is truly the source and summit of all that we are and of all that we hope to become. The Eucharist must be for us a way of life.

"You Left Us Yourself as Food"

SAINT CATHERINE OF SIENA

I taly in the fourteenth century was a place of chaos and confusion for society and for the Church. Socially, it was a time of feuds among the city-states themselves, and between those states and Church authorities; class conflict was almost a norm; poverty was widespread and the plague was claiming many lives. Ecclesiastically, the papacy was exiled from Rome, situated in Avignon, France; the Crusades were underway, fueled by religious passion and cultural intolerance; and the Church was as much involved in forging solutions for society as it was in facilitating the salvation of souls. It was a time with no clear sense of direction for the future.

Into this tumultuous context, in 1347, is born Caterina di Giacomo di Benincasa, more popularly known as Saint Catherine of Siena. Characterizing this Doctor of the Church is no easy task. She is recognized as a mystic by the integrity of her life as a Third Order Dominican and by the depth of wisdom evident in her major writing, *The Dialogue*, in her prayers and in her extensive correspondence. Catherine is also apostolic, even activist. She was involved in the most urgent social and ecclesial issues of her day: feuds between states, service to the poor and to victims of the plague, fidelity of the clergy, the Crusades, papal authority, institutional reform. Whether addressing prince or prelate, she was never afraid to speak her mind, proclaiming the truth of God's Word as it had been revealed to her.

Saint Catherine demonstrates a healthy balance between action and contemplation. She is never too busy to pray. No social prowess or theological precision sustained her in the midst of the many responsibilities and activities which filled her life. Even if she had had the benefits of formal education she would have claimed neither prowess nor precision. She recognized that only a vibrant and vital relationship with the Lord prompted her and provided the stamina and sensitivity she needed to accomplish all that her country and the Church challenged her to do. That relationship with the Lord included concerns and hopes for the society and Church in which she lived, as well as the cares and aspirations of those she encountered. Her participation in the sacramental life of the Church was foundational to her relationship with the Lord.

This chapter focuses on the insights which Saint Catherine of Siena passes on to us concerning the great gift of the Eucharist, "the treasure, the holy sacrament" (*The Dialogue*, chap. 133), which sustained her throughout life.

"I gave you this food"

In referring to the Eucharist as food, Saint Catherine echoes a fundamental teaching presented by Jesus himself. "Those who eat my flesh and drink my blood have eternal life, and I will raise them up on the last day; for my flesh is true food and my blood is true drink" (John 6:54-55). As food, the Eucharist is basic nourishment for the Christian life; Catherine builds upon this teaching to highlight the essential qualities of this food. Her writing reflects God speaking to her:

My deep charity gave him to you as food for your salvation and for your nourishment in this life where you are pilgrim travelers, so that you would have refreshment and would not forget the blessing of the blood. I in my divine providence gave you this food, my gentle Truth, to help you in your need. (*Ibid.*, chap. 112)

As usual, Catherine is straightforward and practical. This food is for salvation and for nourishment, and both are necessary. We are travelers; we are on a journey. The extent of the journey and the distractions that we will inevitably encounter along the way can tire us and distort our reasons for making the journey. This food refreshes us as we continue on our way, reminding us of all that Jesus has done for us through the Paschal Mystery. This refreshment and reminder are evidence of God's providence to us; they are the Truth of God's care for us.

Truth is a major theme in Saint Catherine's spirituality; it is among her favorite names for God and Christ. It expresses her experience of God in whom there can be found no trace of deceit or duplicity. The Eucharist as God's "gentle Truth" guides

us securely on our journey and provides the sustenance we need. We encounter and are nourished
by this Truth each time we participate in the Eucharist. This gentle Truth is a significant means
through which God's transforming work unfolds
within us. This Truth must be the object of our
desire.

Saint Catherine's prayer reflects this same perspective; the Eucharist expresses God's continuing presence among us and strengthens us for the
journey:

> O boundless charity! Just as you gave us
> yourself, wholly God and wholly human,
> so you left us all of yourself as food so
> that while we are pilgrims in this life we
> might not collapse in our weariness but
> be strengthened by you, heavenly food.
> O mercenary people! And what has your
> God left you? He has left you himself,
> wholly God and wholly human, hidden
> under the whiteness of this bread. O fire
> of love! Was it not enough to gift us with
> creation in your image and likeness, and
> to create us anew in grace in your Son's
> blood, without giving us yourself as food,

the whole of divine being, the whole of
God? What drove you? Nothing but your
charity, mad with love as you are! (*Prayers*,
10:24-45)

God's love for us is extravagant. In the Eucharist
we are touched by a "boundless charity" and the
"fire of love." This love has gifted us first by our
creation in God's image and likeness; then by cre-
ating us anew through the life and death of Jesus;
and now by giving us food which sustains us. Creation, Incarnation, Salvation, Eucharist — such is
the expansive nature of God's constant and continuing love for us. This can only be the work of
one who is "mad with love."

In societies where food is accessible and plen-
tiful, it can be taken for granted. The same reality
can color our relationship with the Eucharist. We
can take for granted or even forget the great love
through which we have received this sublime gift.
Saint Catherine recognizes the need to focus on
and to explore the immensity of God's gracious-
ness to us and love for us:

You want me to contemplate your gift
to me — your gift of creation in your
image and likeness. In that creation, su-

preme eternal purity, you joined yourself with the mire of our humanity. You
were driven by the fire of your charity,
and with that same fire you left us yourself
as food. (*Ibid.*, 12:71-82)

We, too, must contemplate this gift. We, too, must
recognize the fire of love which created us, became
like us, and continues to sustain us through the
Eucharist. We, too, must eat this food and be transformed in God.

"The soul is in God"

Jesus indicates the close connection between
the Eucharist as food and as a means of union with
him. "Those who eat my flesh and drink my blood
abide in me and I in them" (John 5:56). The Eucharist is a powerful support and a pure source of
nourishment for our life. It is yet more. Through
the Eucharist we cultivate a lasting intimacy with
God. From Saint Catherine's perspective, the Eucharist draws us into an intense union with God.

"In communion the soul seems more sweetly
bound to God and better knows his truth. For then
the soul is in God and God in the soul, just as the
fish is in the sea and the sea is in the fish" (*The*

Dialogue, chap. 2). This brief text articulates eloquently an important principle for understanding the primary effects of the Eucharist on which Catherine comments later in her writing. The principle is basic. By baptism and through our participation in the Christian community and by our efforts to live the mission and message of Jesus, the soul is already united to God and knows God's truth. This union and knowledge reflect the Christian character of our life. It is our responsibility, in cooperation with God's grace, to advance that union and knowledge.

There is an intensity in the Eucharist which strengthens that character, deepening our intimacy with God and sharpening our understanding of God's ways. Our participation in the Eucharist nurtures inseparability from God and familiarity with God. In commenting on the effects of the Eucharist which flow from all this, Saint Catherine builds upon the basic principle:

> Contemplate the marvelous state of the soul who receives this bread of life, this food of angels.... When she receives this sacrament she lives in me and I in her.... Grace lives in such a soul because, hav-

ing received this bread of life in grace, she lives in grace. When this appearance of bread has been consumed, I leave behind the imprint of my grace, just as a seal that is pressed into warm wax leaves its imprint when it is lifted off. Thus does the power of the sacrament remain there in the soul; that is, the warmth of my divine charity, the mercy of the Holy Spirit, remains there. The light of my only-begotten Son's wisdom remains there, enlightening the mind's eye. The soul is left strong, sharing in my strength and power, which make her strong and powerful against her selfish sensuality and against the devil and the world. (*Ibid.*, chap. 112)

According to Saint Catherine, the work of the Eucharist within us is extensive. First, she reiterates the union between God and the soul which takes place during communion: "she lives in me and I in her." As she has noted earlier, these encounters with the Lord form the foundation upon which a lasting union and intimacy are built. Second, the soul "lives in grace." Participation in the Eucharist calls us to holiness, to live by God's grace in all we do. Third, we are imprinted by that grace which conveys power to us. Specifically, that power is "the warmth of divine charity, the mercy of the Holy Spirit, … the light of my only begotten Son's wisdom." This love and mercy and wisdom must become the hallmarks of our life if we are to be known as followers of Jesus and as people of the Eucharist. Fourth, "the soul is left strong" with the Lord's own strength, enabling us to remain faithful in response to whatever could compromise our relationship with God. Fidelity reflects our desire for and our commitment to that relationship.

These effects of the Eucharist, these qualities which remain, will develop only if they are lived, only if they are brought into our ordinary tasks and responsibilities, only if they mark our encounters and relationships with others. Union, holiness, love, mercy, wisdom, fidelity — these are the qualities by which we will be transformed into the likeness of Jesus; these qualities confirm that "the soul is in God and God in the soul" not only when we participate in the Eucharist, but throughout our life.

"With affectionate love"

"You must receive this sacrament not only with your bodily senses but with your spiritual sensitivity, by disposing your soul to see and receive and taste this sacrament with affectionate love" (*The Dialogue*, chap. 111). Our participation in the Eucharist engages every aspect of our humanity. Most certainly the physical dimension of our life, the "bodily senses," are involved because of the materials consumed. Quite literally, the body and blood of Christ become part of the very fiber of our physical constitution. Saint Catherine reminds us, though, that our "spiritual sensitivity" is the key means through which we receive the full benefits of this sacrament. We must be disposed to receive the Eucharist; we must prepare ourselves. That disposition and preparation must be characterized and driven by love, by a true affection for the Lord. Apart from that love, the Eucharist can become for us merely a ritual meal with little real significance for and influence on our spiritual growth and development. How can we dispose ourselves, then, "to see and receive and taste this sacrament with affectionate love"?

"What tastes and sees and touches this sacrament? The soul's sensitivity. How does she see it? With her mind's eye, so long as it has the pupil of holy faith" (*ibid.*). We see the Eucharist by faith; thus, we accept and acknowledge the body and blood of the Lord present in this sacrament. Apart from that faith we see but bread and wine. From Saint Catherine's perspective, the eyes of faith are sharper and more discerning than our physical sense of sight. She teaches us that "the spiritual must be the principal vision, because it cannot be deceived. It is with this eye, then, that you must contemplate this sacrament" (*ibid.*). Physical sight can be deceived. We can choose to see what we want, easily misleading our senses and ourselves. Faith is not so easily duped. We may not accept or be comfortable with the truth which our spiritual sight places before us, but we do not thereby reconfigure that truth according to our preferences. As we become people of the Eucharist, faith must become our primary mode of sight and interpretation. Saint Paul teaches us, "we walk by faith, not by sight" (2 Corinthians 5:7). Such faith will guide us more surely than any other vision, however sharp it may be.

"How is this sacrament touched? With the hand of love. This hand it is that touches what the eye has seen and known in this sacrament. The hand of love touches through faith, confirming as it were what the soul sees and knows spiritually through faith" (*ibid.*). Love builds upon faith, enabling us to encounter Jesus in the Eucharist. We touch in love what we see by faith. If we do not see with the eyes of faith, then we touch but bread and wine. Saint Catherine recognizes the intimacy into which we are invited through our participation in this sacrament. Her teaching here echoes the opening words of Saint John's first letter: "We declare to you what was from the beginning, what we have heard, what we have seen with our eyes, what we have looked at and touched with our hands, concerning the word of life" (1 John 1:1). We touch with love what we see by faith. The Eucharist gives us an unparalleled opportunity for closeness to Jesus. We encounter Jesus with love and so are built up in love and gradually become people of love.

"How is this sacrament tasted? With holy desire. The body tastes only the flavor of bread, but the soul tastes me, God and human" (*ibid.*). We taste through longing what we touch in love and see by faith. Our relationship with Jesus in the Eucharist must be more than obligation; we must desire to see and touch and taste the Lord. We must long to be one with Jesus, we must want the Lord to be a part of our life. It is only through our desire for this union that we can taste the depth of God's love for us in the Eucharist. There is power in human desire and that power is a gift of our creation. God does not use force in drawing us into union. God invites us, we must want and choose to respond; we must desire to live the fullness of God's gift to us. Apart from that desire, our life can lack focus and direction; we will miss the opportunities for union that God offers to us. To be alert for those opportunities, everything in the spiritual life must be done "with holy desire."

Saint Catherine summarizes her teaching by indicating the inherent collaboration among the faith, love, and desire with which we must approach the Eucharist:

> The body's senses can be deceived, but not the soul's. In fact, they confirm and clarify the matter for her, for what the mind's eye has seen and known through the pupil of holy faith, she touches with the hand of love. What she has seen she touches in love and faith. And she tastes it with her spiritual sense of holy desire, that is, she tastes the burning, unspeakable charity with which I have made her worthy to receive the tremendous mystery of this sacrament and its grace. (*ibid.*)

Thus do we develop and mature in our capacity to

approach and receive the Eucharist "with affectionate love."

"According to the desire of those who receive it"

The Eucharist is a gift to us, yet its effect on us can be neither assumed nor taken for granted. If such were the case, we could receive the sacrament as disinterested bystanders and our growth in the spiritual life would be automatically assured. The reality, however, is that the quality and character of our desire for and response to this gift of the Eucharist have a key role in determining the extent of its effects on our spiritual development. Saint Catherine's teaching is direct:

> This food gives more or less strength according to the desire of those who receive it, whether they receive it sacramentally or virtually. "Sacramentally" is when one communicates in the holy Sacrament. "Virtually" is communicating through holy desire, both in longing for communion and in esteem for the blood of Christ crucified. (*The Dialogue*, chap. 66)

Catherine does not create an arbitrary distinction of intensity between the modes by which we can receive the Eucharist as if one would have a greater impact upon us regardless of our approach to it. Whether our reception of the Eucharist is "sacramental" or "virtual," our desire for this encounter with the Lord remains the key component in strengthening and deepening our relationship with Jesus. This teaching challenges us to examine regularly the quality of our preparation for and participation in the Eucharist. Our disposition does makes a difference.

Saint Catherine teaches us that the benefits available to us in the Eucharist are not limited by our capability and capacity to receive them. That capability and capacity are gifts to human nature by our creation in God's image and likeness. Any benefits from the Eucharist can be limited, however, by the quality of our desire to choose and embrace them:

> It is with love that you come to receive my gracious glorious light, the light I have given you as food, to be administered to you by my ministers. But even though all of you receive the light, each of you receives it in proportion to the love and burning desire you bring with you....

Each of you carries the light whole and undivided, for it cannot be divided by any imperfection in you who receive it or in those who administer it. You share as much of the light (that is, the grace you receive in this sacrament) as your holy desire disposes you to receive. (*Ibid.*)

The light to which Catherine refers is nothing less than the fire of God's love and truth. We are transformed by that fire "more or less intensely depending on the material (we bring) to this flame" (*ibid.*). We will never be ignited by God's love if the material we bring to the fire of that love is not marked by a passion and desire for the transformation to which it invites us. The choice is ours; our disposition will determine what we receive.

"Each of you can grow in love and virtue as you choose and as I give you grace" (*ibid.*). Our continuing spiritual development, our growth in love and virtue, progresses through the interaction of our free will and God's grace. Both are necessary: free will, because God works by cooperation not coercion; grace, so we will advance with direction and by discernment. The Eucharist facilitates the workings of that grace and fashions our will according to God's own. Our participation in the Eucharist is a privilege in which we share by our baptism and our initiation into the Body of Christ. It is also a responsibility we bear, an action which must engage us fully. We must embrace this privilege and accept this responsibility if the Eucharist is to be a means of growth for us. Truly, this sacrament accomplishes the work of transformation "according to the desire of those who receive it."

"You are table and food and waiter"

We encounter the Lord Jesus in the Eucharist, and so we encounter the Trinity. We are thus drawn into the life of the Trinity and share in the gifts promised to us in baptism and by our incorporation into the Body of Christ. We have been invited to the banquet of the Eucharist, we are the guests. The role that Saint Catherine identifies for the Trinity at this banquet is service. In her *Prayers*, she says:

> I shall clothe myself in your eternal will, and by this light I shall come to know that you, eternal Trinity, are table and food and waiter for us. You, eternal Father, are the table that offers us as food the Lamb, your only-begotten Son. He

is the most exquisite of foods for us, both
in his teaching which nourishes us in your
will, and in the sacrament that we receive
in holy communion, which feeds and
strengthens us while we are pilgrim travelers in this life. And the Holy Spirit is
indeed a waiter for us, for he serves us
this teaching by enlightening our mind's
eye with it and inspiring us to follow it.
(12:126-147)

In responding to such extravagance, we must come
to the table, consume the food, and commend the
waiter. We must enter into this relationship with
the Trinity and accept the generous service extended
to us, for its end is our transformation.

Saint Catherine's perspective on the Eucharist, like her spirituality, is eminently practical. It
calls us to action, to take responsibility, to apply
our faith in all the events of daily life. The Eucharist invites us into a lively intimacy with God, sustained and strengthened by the faith, love, and desire
with which we approach this sacrament. The quality
of our disposition and the character of our participation serve as gauges for the extent to which this
sacrament will touch and transform our life. The
Eucharist is our nourishment for the spiritual life,

for following the Lord Jesus with integrity and intimacy, with purpose and passion. Lord, may we be ever grateful for that nourishment and recognize the great gift you have given to us when, in your love for us, "you left us yourself as food." May our life be flavored with that food, always welcoming the work of your transforming grace within us, and longing to live with you forever. Amen.

"Delight and Consolation in the Most Blessed Sacrament"

SAINT TERESA OF AVILA

We move now from fourteenth-century Italy to sixteenth-century Spain. It was the Age of Discovery. Physical geography was being redrawn by the voyages of Columbus, Magellan and others. Humanity's knowledge and understanding of the world were expanding. Spiritual geography was being redrawn also by the work of spiritual writers and theologians. Christians' knowledge and understanding of the spiritual life were deepening. Both geographies were becoming more precise. It was a time of almost unlimited horizons and Spain was among the leaders in all this, on the sea and in the soul.

Into this adventurous time, in 1515, is born Teresa Sanchez Cepeda Davila y Ahumada, more commonly known as Saint Teresa of Avila. Her name as a Carmelite religious was Sister Teresa of Jesus. Her influence upon and significance within the mystical tradition of the Church has remained firm over these past four centuries. As a Doctor of the Church, her writings and teachings have been a source of wisdom, guidance, and inspiration for countless individuals. Admirers and students of her thinking can be found in every culture and religion.

Too often it is assumed that the topics which Saint Teresa addresses in her writings are highly specialized and limited to mystical states and extraordinary phenomena. As a member of the Church, however, Teresa is one of us; her own spiritual life was built upon and nurtured by her participation in the liturgical, sacramental, and devotional prayers and practices of the Church. It should be no surprise, then, to discover that Teresa offers to us a perspective on the Eucharist. Very simply, there is "delight and consolation in the most Blessed Sacrament" (*Way of Perfection*, 34:2).

"Ardent desires to receive communion"

The primary lens through which Saint Teresa views the Eucharist is her own experience.

Though there are instances in her writings that reflect a theological and doctrinal understanding of the Blessed Sacrament, her perspective usually reflects her own experiences of encountering the Lord Jesus in the Eucharist. By drawing upon those experiences, Teresa can refer to this sacrament in a variety of ways. At times she speaks of the Eucharist as a point of reference for some significant event in her life. In the *Book of her Life*, she recounts the beginning of the first convent she founded. "One day after Communion, His Majesty earnestly commanded me to strive for this new monastery with all my powers" (32:11). Whether she speaks of insights received or actions to be taken or accomplishments to be celebrated, Teresa often frames such happenings in the context of their proximity to her participation in and reception of the Eucharist.

At other times, especially when circumstances made it difficult for her to receive the Eucharist, Saint Teresa speaks of her intense longing for the sacrament. "On occasion there come over me such ardent desires to receive Communion that I don't think they could be exaggerated" (*Life*, 39:2). Precisely because the Eucharist was a reference point in Teresa's life, marking moments when the Lord was especially present and active in her experience, the prospect that she might not have access to this sacrament was particularly distressing.

At still other times, Teresa recognizes that the material which the Lord chose for the Eucharist makes this encounter less daunting. Because of our human weakness, it would be difficult for us to bear an encounter with the resurrected and glorified Lord Jesus if he was visibly present as such in the Eucharist. Teresa writes, "there is no person capable of enduring such a glorious sight.... Beneath that bread he is easy to deal with" (*Way*, 34:9). Bread is so ordinary, so familiar, that we do not hesitate to approach even the risen and glorified Lord.

Saint Teresa's references to and descriptions of the Eucharist reflect the fundamental truth underlying her experience — in this sacrament we encounter the Lord Jesus. That encounter is a reality and a reminder. In the Eucharist we participate in the reality of receiving the Lord, who nourishes us and strengthens us as we strive to communicate his message and continue his mission. In the Eucharist also is the reminder that the Lord is ever present and active in our life and in our world. Such a reality and reminder invite us and even urge us to "find delight and consolation in the most Blessed Sacrament" (*Way*, 34:2).

"Grow accustomed to having him present"

Saint Teresa's book, *Way of Perfection*, is a primer in the spiritual life. As she went about the business of founding convents, she realized that some of those entering religious life needed basic instruction and encouragement in the spiritual life. The *Way*, then, was written from the practical perspective of offering advice and guidance for beginning and maintaining the life of prayer.

In chapters twenty-six through forty-two, Teresa presents her reflections on the Lord's Prayer. Her purpose is not analytical, but pastoral; she places the challenge before us:

> If you can grow accustomed to having him present at your side, and he sees that you do so with love and that you go about striving to please him, you will not be able — as they say — to get away from him; he will never fail you; he will help you in your trials; you will find him everywhere. (*Way*, 26:1)

Praying the Our Father reflectively facilitates our attentiveness to the Lord. Beginning with chapter twenty-seven, Teresa comments on the Lord's Prayer phrase by phrase.

In chapters thirty-three through thirty-five, she focuses on the phrase "Give us today our daily bread." She understands this "bread" to be the Eucharist and so her comments unfold accordingly. Though Saint Teresa speaks of the Eucharist in her other writings, these three chapters in the *Way of Perfection* represent her thinking in its most concentrated form.

"A means was necessary"

"Your will be done on earth as it is in heaven." We pray this phrase so often that it is ever at risk of becoming words with no weight. However, when we take the time to reflect on the task of completing God's will in our daily life, we discover that it is indeed a weighty matter to pray such words seriously and sincerely. They represent what we claim we will do and what we promise to do. It is challenging to be faithful in completing God's will throughout life; yet that is precisely what we pray. Jesus has given us an example of living in fidelity to God's will. Still, that example does not necessarily make the task before us any less difficult. The Lord well understands all this, as Saint Teresa reminds us:

> The Lord knows our weakness, that we often show we do not understand what the Lord's will is. We are weak and he is merciful. He knows that a means was necessary. He saw it would not be in any way to our benefit if we failed to give what he gave, because all our gain lies in giving this. He saw that doing the Father's will was difficult. (*Way*, 33:1)

Jesus' recognition of this situation is not passive; rather, he responds to our need with the gift of himself:

> Now then, once Jesus saw the need, he sought out a wonderful means by which to show the extreme of his love for us, and in his own name and in that of his brothers he made the following petition: "Give us this day, Lord, our daily bread." (*Ibid.*)

Our relationship with the Lord through the Eucharist and our union with the Lord in the Eucharist are the means we need to be constant and consistent in completing God's will. The gift of the Eucharist represents "the extreme of his love for us." We could not have construed or constructed a more powerful means of support.

The principal challenge here is whether we recognize our own weakness, whether we acknowledge our need for a means to assist us in completing God's will. The Eucharist reminds us that we are not self-contained, we are not resources unto ourselves. Even with such a reminder, we may continue to perceive ourselves as self-sufficient. And we may even practice that by neglecting to utilize the very means that the Lord has provided for us. This perception and practice need the transforming touch of God's grace. Without that transformation we can live as if we do not need God. Such a life insulates us from the full effects of God's presence and activity. Such a life reflects an arrogance and pride which corrode our sensitivity to God's will and constrict the significance we assign to our relationship with the Lord.

The Lord remains ever faithful, even when confronted with the prospect of our infidelity. Saint Teresa's words are realistic and encouraging:

> Jesus observed what he had given for us,
> how important it was that we in turn give
> this, and the great difficulty there is in
> our doing so, as we said, since we are the
> way we are: inclined to base things and
> with so little love and courage that it was
> necessary for us to see his love and courage
> in order to be awakened — and not just
> once but every day. After he saw all this,
> he must have resolved to remain with us
> here below. (*Way*, 33:2)

It is as Jesus had promised: "I am with you always;
yes, even to the end of time" (Matthew 28:20). The
Eucharist is the fulfillment of that promise.

"One with us here below"

Jesus remains among us, but not as a casual
and distant observer. Indeed, he becomes one with
us and identifies with us. He experienced what we
experience, he struggled as we struggle. Scripture
testifies to this:

> He had to become like his brothers and
> sisters in every respect so that he might
> be a merciful and faithful high priest in

the service of God.... Because he himself was tested by what he suffered, he is able to help those who are being saved. (Hebrews 2:17-28)

Later on, the author of the Letter to the Hebrews is even more emphatic: "We do not have a high priest who is unable to sympathize with our weaknesses, but we have one who in every respect has been tested as we are, yet without sin" (4:15). This is Jesus who becomes one with us in the Eucharist.

Jesus identifies with us. For Saint Teresa, this union through identification is a profound truth which challenges us to be ever attentive to the quality of our response:

> Since by sharing in our nature he has become one with us here below — and as Lord of his own will — he reminds the Father that because he belongs to him the Father in turn can give him to us. And so he says, "our bread." He doesn't make any difference between himself and us, but we make one by not giving ourselves up each day for His Majesty. (*Way*, 33:5)

Jesus' desire is that there be no "difference between himself and us." To fulfill that desire he gave himself for us even unto death. He remains among us and identifies with us by becoming our daily bread.

Why, then, is there a distance and a difference between ourselves and the Lord? We make and maintain that distance and difference "by not giving ourselves up each day" for the Lord. Our response to the gift of the Eucharist must be nothing less than the death to self that Jesus modeled for us in his living response to God's will. Jesus gives himself that we may learn to give ourselves; his fidelity to God's will is the standard that we must embrace in our discernment and discovery of God's will for us.

Jesus' presence to us and union with us in the Eucharist are multifaceted from Teresa's perspective.

First, Jesus in the Eucharist is a source of strength and encouragement. In fact, as Teresa tells us, "There is no need or trial or persecution that is not easy to suffer if we begin to enjoy the delight and consolation of this sacred bread" (*Way*, 34:2). Because Jesus identifies with us and is one with us in the Eucharist, there is a familiarity and a comfortability in our sharing of the Eucharist. Teresa does not say the need or trial or persecution will be taken away. It will not, for it is our cross and we must carry it. Rather, the Eucharist provides strength for the journey. The Eucharist is also a source of encouragement when all that we see and know is the cross, when all that we experience is distance from the Lord:

> We have him so near in the Blessed Sacrament, where he is already glorified and where we don't have to gaze upon him as being so tired and worn out, bleeding, wearied by his journeys.... Behold him here without suffering, full of glory, before ascending into heaven, strengthening some, encouraging others, our companion in the most Blessed Sacrament; it doesn't seem it was in his power to leave us for even a moment.... The Lord helps us, strengthens us, and never fails; he is a true friend. (*Life*, 22:6)

Second, Jesus in the Eucharist is a source of peace and healing. The turbulence in our world and in our own life can become overwhelming at times, dulling our awareness of God's peaceful and healing presence and activity. Saint Teresa relates the definite influence that the Eucharist had on her own life experience. "Sometimes (or almost ordinarily — at least, quite often) after receiving Communion I was at peace. And sometimes in approaching the Sacrament I felt at once so good in soul and body that I was surprised" (*Life*, 30:14). And again, "I have experienced for more than a half year that at least when I am receiving Communion I noticeably and clearly feel bodily health" (*Spiritual Testimonies*, 1:23). The Eucharist was a source of peace and healing for Teresa even in the midst of loneliness. She recounts, "All day yesterday I felt very lonely, except for when I received Communion I benefitted little from the fact that it was Easter Sunday" (*ibid.*, 12:1). Our experience will not necessarily parallel Teresa's own. We bear the responsibility of identifying the distinctive impact that the Eucharist has on our life with all its ups and downs. The challenge is to explore our own relationship with Jesus in the Eucharist, to discover the peace and healing that are offered to us through that relationship.

Third, Jesus in the Eucharist is present and accessible. The Eucharist reflects the great truth of the Incarnation — God is with us. We cannot relegate the life and mission of Jesus to the annals of history, revering them as noble accomplishments of the past. Jesus' life and mission, teaching and healing continue even now. The Lord is ever present and accessible. In writing about her reaction to those who lock Jesus into a single historical period, Saint Teresa recounts:

> The Lord had given her such living faith that when she heard some persons saying they would have liked to have lived at the time that Christ our Good walked in the world, she used to laugh to herself. She wondered what more they wanted since in the most Blessed Sacrament they had him just as truly present as he was then. (*Way*, 34:6)

Because the Eucharist is so accessible, as ordinary as daily bread, it is easy for us to take it for granted. Occasionally, we can lose sight of the great gift that is always accessible to us. "For although we often do not take note, it ought to be a great consolation for us that Jesus Christ, true God and true man, is present in the most Blessed Sacrament in many places" (*The Foundations*, 18:5). The key is for us to "take note" of Jesus' continuing presence and activity among us and his constant accessibility to us.

Jesus remains among us and identifies with us. This is the work of the Incarnation, this is the gift of the Eucharist. We need not look elsewhere; the Lord is before us, inviting us to be one with him:

> Receiving Communion is not like picturing with the imagination, as when we reflect upon the Lord on the cross or in other episodes of the Passion, when we picture within ourselves how things happened to him in the past. In Communion the event is happening now, and it is entirely true. There's no reason to go looking for him in some other place farther away.... Now, then, if when he went about in the world the mere touch of his robes cured the sick, why doubt, if we have faith, that miracles will be worked while he is within us and that he will give what we ask of him, since he is in our house? His Majesty is not accustomed to paying poorly for his lodging if the hospitality is good. (*Way*, 34:8)

How can we assure that our "hospitality is good"?

"Do not abandon this practice"

The recommendations which Saint Teresa passes on to us are simple. Two are primary. The first concerns our approach to the Eucharist; that is, our preparation for receiving Communion. The second recommendation focuses on the importance of recollection after receiving Communion. More than mere practices which precede and follow our participation in the Eucharist, these recommendations constitute a means of formation for our spiritual life.

As for our preparation, Teresa instructs us to ask the Lord "to give (us) the dispositions to receive him worthily" (*Way*, 34:3). The essential dispositions for approaching the Eucharist worthily are to set our heart on the Lord, to desire to do all things for the Lord, and to surrender to God's will in everything. In other words, to find our "delight and consolation in the most Blessed Sacrament" (*Way*, 34:2). In her usual style, Teresa is direct. "Your attitude should be like that of a servant when he begins to serve. His care is about pleasing his master in everything" (*Way*, 34:5). We can set our heart on the Lord only if we truly trust that the Lord loves us and will provide for us. The alternative is to expend much time and energy on realities that we cannot control. Therefore, "let us watch so that we don't advertently place our care on anything other than begging the Lord for what I have mentioned; in having this, we will have everything" (*Way*, 34:5).

Our sense of familiarity and comfortability with the Eucharist is something of a two-edged sword. On the one hand we can approach the Eucharist easily and regularly; the Lord is present and accessible and extends to us strength and encouragement, peace and healing. On the other hand that familiarity and comfortability can lull us into an occasional forgetfulness of the significance of this encounter with the Lord:

> I think that if we were to approach the most Blessed Sacrament with great faith and love, once would be enough to leave us rich. How much richer from approaching so many times as we do. The trouble is we do so out of routine, and it shows. (*Meditations on the Song of Songs*, 3:13)

The key is evident, we must approach the Eucharist "with great faith and love." These qualities and gifts from God do not make all aspects of the "routine" disappear, but they can refocus our attention and refresh our understanding of the significance of our encounter with Jesus in the Eucharist.

Saint Teresa's second recommendation concerns the time immediately following our reception of Communion. This is an especially important moment; all our attention should be fixed on the Lord who is within us:

> Be with him willingly; don't lose so good an occasion for conversing with him as is the hour after having received Communion.... If you immediately turn your thoughts to other things, if you pay no attention and take no account of the fact that he is within you, how will he be able to reveal himself to you? This, then, is a good time for our Master to teach us, and for us to listen to him, kiss his feet because he wanted to teach us, and beg him not to leave. (*Way*, 34:10)

Our preparation for and approach to the Eucharist form a single weaving with this period after Communion. If we have prepared and approached with faith and love, we might not be so quick to turn our thoughts to other things afterwards. This is indeed a good time to listen, to learn, to be strengthened for the spiritual journey. It is a graced time that we should use to be with the Lord.

Teresa offers some further advice:

> After having received the Lord, since you have the Person himself present, strive to close the eyes of the body and open those of the soul and look into your heart. For I tell you, and tell you again, and would like to tell you many times that you should acquire the habit of doing this every time you receive Communion. (*Way*, 34:12)

We know well enough that we will soon be dealing with the barrage of tasks and responsibilities that fill our daily life. The moments we take after Communion can be a time of rest, refreshment, and revitalization. Very often, the greatest challenges before us are those within our ordinary, everyday activities. Our daily interactions with family, friends, co-workers, and others are the arena in which we confirm or contradict the sincerity and seriousness of our desire and efforts to live the mission and message of Jesus. The Eucharist nurtures that desire and supports those efforts. Thus, in speaking of recollection after Communion, Saint Teresa insists: "Do not abandon this practice; the Lord will see in it how much you love him" (*Way*, 35:2).

"What greater good could I want?"

Saint Teresa of Avila's perspective on the Eucharist, though not primarily doctrinal, does reflect the Church's understanding of this sacrament. The Eucharist is an extension of the Incarnation. In exploring and reflecting on her own experience, Teresa realized that the completion of God's will requires a means of support. For, left to our own devices and resources, we might never do what we promise as we pray the words that Jesus taught us — "Your will be done." The Eucharist draws us into an ever-deepening intimacy with the Lord precisely so we can fulfill God's will in our life even as Jesus fulfilled that will in his own:

> Here on earth we possess him and also in heaven we will possess him if we profit well by his company. He, in fact, doesn't remain with us for any other reason than to help, encourage, and sustain us in doing this will that we have prayed might be done in us. (*Way*, 34:1)

The Eucharist spans time. It is rooted in the historical life and work of Jesus of Nazareth; it is celebrated now in Jesus' continuing presence and activity among us; and it will be fulfilled in eternal life, our complete union with God. Through the Eucharist we share in the timelessness of God and in the very life of God:

> And what greater good could I want in this life than to be so close to You, that there be no division between You and me? With this companionship, what can be difficult? What can not one undertake for You, being so closely joined? (*Meditations on the Song of Songs*, 4:9)

Saint Teresa of Avila gives us a glimpse into all that God offers to us through the "delight and consolation in the most Blessed Sacrament" (*Way*, 34:2). The challenge we must take up and the responsibility we bear are to remain close to the Lord who loves us, who has chosen us, and who becomes "our daily bread." We must desire and choose to remain close to the Lord who wants to nourish us and accompany us as we continue along the pathways of our spiritual journey.

"The Soul Receives Joy and Gladness"

SAINT JOHN OF THE CROSS

For this chapter we will remain in the same time and place that we visited in the preceding one, sixteenth-century Spain. We will shift our attention, however, to the Discalced Carmelite religious whose life and work are most closely associated with those of Saint Teresa of Avila. Juan de Yepes was born in 1542; we know him as Saint John of the Cross. This Doctor of the Church is both a mystic and a theologian of the mystical life. As a priest and celebrant, he had access to the Eucharist on a daily basis, affording him ample opportunities to reflect on this encounter with the Lord Jesus and on its significance for his life. Such access is noteworthy when we recall that, except for ordained ministers, the regular reception of Communion was rare in Spain and elsewhere, almost until the early twentieth century when Pope

Saint Pius X emphasized the importance of frequent Communion for all Catholics.

Like Saint Teresa, John of the Cross offers us a perspective on the Eucharist. It is shaped by his training as a theologian, his spiritual life as a Carmelite, and his personal experience of relationship with the Lord. He recognized and experienced — and teaches us — that, in the Eucharist, "the soul receives joy and gladness" (*Dark Night*, Book I, 4:2).

The Spiritual Life

The basic perspective with which Saint John of the Cross approaches the Eucharist is as a theologian of the spiritual life. Though his teaching reflects his own experience, rare are the instances in which he elaborates on that experience as an example. Rather, he uses his theological expertise and precision as a means of guiding and encouraging his readers to explore their own experiences, to discover the Lord there. In today's terms, it could be said that Saint John invites readers to internalize and integrate his teaching in light of their own spiritual journey and, in particular, their relationship with the Eucharist.

It is beyond the scope of this chapter to provide a full overview of sanjuanist spirituality. However, it can be said that Saint John's goal is to lead the person toward full union with God alone. The key word here is "alone." The spiritual life is a gradual process of transformation toward that union, and anything which would disrupt or delay that process must be removed from our life. This process of detachment is extensive, encompassing every dimension of our life — internal and external. It affects our physical senses — sight, hearing, taste, touch, smell; and our spiritual senses — intellect, memory, imagination, will. The process involves what we can do to facilitate our journey; that is, the active aspects of the spiritual life. And it involves what only the Lord can do within us; that is, the passive aspects of the spiritual life.

All is done to cultivate our union with God. Our very identity must be rooted in God alone. Everything else in our life is valued in light of our desire to be one with God and our efforts to fulfill that desire. Whatever does not strengthen that desire holds the potential to sabotage it. Thus, the theme of detachment is foundational to a clear understanding of Saint John's teaching.

John of the Cross comments on the Eucharist in several contexts within his writings. Those contexts correspond to our growth and development along the pathways of our spiritual journey.

"Benefit from it only for the sake of going to God"

A major task in the spiritual life — if not the major task — is directing our will toward unity with God and conformity to God's will. All our senses — physical and spiritual — influence the will and so can hasten or hinder that direction. Disciplining our senses, purifying them, comprises a major portion of the active aspects of the spiritual life. Assuredly, the Lord is at work always, but our efforts to focus our entire life on the Lord, through the input we receive from our senses, are evidence of the priorities we have established by choice. They are evidence that we are directing our will toward union with God. This is one context in which Saint John of the Cross mentions the Eucharist.

In Book Three of his spiritual classic, *Ascent of Mount Carmel*, Saint John is addressing the active dimensions of the purification process within the spiritual journey. The challenge is to focus on God's presence and activity through our sense-experiences. He writes:

Whenever spiritual persons, on hearing music or other things, seeing agreeable objects, smelling sweet fragrance, or feeling the delight of certain tastes and delicate touches, immediately at the first movement direct their thought and the affection of their will to God, receiving more satisfaction in the thought of God than in the sensible object that caused it. (*Ascent*, III, 24:5)

The beauty and goodness that we sense and experience through all of creation are indicators of God's own beauty and goodness. When we choose to remain fixed on the created object rather than the Creator, those realities which require faith and which are not particularly satisfying to the senses will be assigned much less significance in our life. Saint John's instruction in response to this is clear. "Spiritual persons, then, in whatever sensory gratification come their way, whether by chance or through their own intention, ought to benefit from it only for the sake of going to God" (*ibid.*, 24:7).

This is the principle of detachment at work. Our experiences can speak to us of God present and active within us and around us. Detachment does not negate the fundamental goodness of created reality; rather, it assures that God remains our highest priority. All else is given value in light of that priority. Detachment does not diminish the delight and joy we experience; rather, it challenges us to embrace them, not only for themselves, but "for the sake of going to God."

The alternative can hinder not only our progress in the spiritual life, but it can skew our perspective regarding the value of those practices specifically intended to hasten our progress. It is precisely here that Saint John comments on the Eucharist. The value of the Eucharist for our continued spiritual progress is unquestionable. That progress can be disrupted, however, if we allow our experience to redirect our attention and so undermine our appreciation for the value of the Eucharist.

John of the Cross speaks of this alternative as spiritual harm. Among the kinds of harm which can result from that diminished appreciation he cites a "decrease in spiritual exercises and corporeal penances, and lukewarmness and lack of devotion in the use of the sacraments of penance and the Eucharist" (*ibid.*, 25:8). Devotion to the Eucharist requires faith; and that faith resides in the will. We must choose to embrace the truth of Jesus' presence in the Eucharist, we must choose to celebrate and receive the Eucharist as a significant means of support for our spiritual life and for all of life.

We can and will have occasions when we sense and experience God's presence and activity within and around us in a heightened way as we participate in the Eucharist. However, those occasions do not become the norm for each time we receive Communion. While they are supportive of our spiritual life, and they are encouraging to us along the way, such occasions cannot become the determining factors upon which we build our fidelity to the Eucharist. Fidelity must be sustained by faith, by that conviction of will through which we choose to return again and again to the Eucharist as a privileged encounter with the Lord; an encounter which transcends any particular sense or experience. Many are the benefits we can receive from the Eucharist; Saint John of the Cross teaches us to desire and to benefit from it, above all, "for the sake of going to God."

"Set the eyes of faith on this invisible grace"

Saint John wrote an accompanying volume to the *Ascent of Mount Carmel* in which he explores the passive dimensions of the purification process. In the *Dark Night*, also a spiritual classic, John focuses on that transformation which only the Lord can accomplish within us. Though it is essential that we welcome and cooperate with the direction in which the Lord leads us, this transformation is essentially the work of grace. Even in this dimension of the spiritual life, there are forces at work which can distract and misguide the will in its desire and search for union with God.

In Book One of the *Dark Night*, John is addressing the passive purification that must take place regarding our sense-experiences if the will is to be truly united with God. He begins by reiterating the teaching he had presented in the *Ascent*. He notes that beginners in the spiritual life are fervent, serious, and sincere in practicing their faith. They are happy to be engaged in the spiritual journey:

> The soul finds its joy in spending lengthy periods at prayer, perhaps even entire nights; its penances are pleasures; its fasts, happiness; and the sacraments and spiritual conversations are its consolations. (*Dark Night*, I, 1:3)

The Eucharist, of course, is among the sacraments as a source of consolation.

Such consolation is an encouragement on the spiritual journey and a stimulant to continue on our way, to look forward to the growth and development that are yet to come. While Saint John acknowledges the importance of taking delight and finding joy in our spiritual practices, he never loses sight of the process by which the will must be purified: detachment. Fervor and joy and delight are characteristic of the initial stages within the spiritual life. Though good, those same characteristics can influence our will to become fixed on the experience itself and neglect attention to the source. Once that happens to those on the journey, "their motivation in their spiritual works and exercises is the consolation and satisfaction they experience in them" (*ibid.*).

The challenge which John of the Cross places before us is to probe ourselves and to determine if the joy we experience in the Eucharist reflects our relationship with the Lord or our own self-satisfaction. Our relationship with the Lord is ever a source of power for the spiritual journey. Self-satisfaction can deteriorate into pride. The strength we receive through the Eucharist is meant to lead us from pride to power, to Jesus as the center of our life.

That we can experience a noticeable joy and delight in our spiritual practices is not surprising. We are body and spirit; both are involved in our journey, both are involved in our relationship with God, both participate in the Eucharist. John acknowledges

> the pleasure human nature finds in spiritual exercises. Since both the spiritual and the sensory parts of the soul receive gratification from that refreshment, each part experiences delight according to its own nature and properties. (*ibid.*, 4:2)

Among the properties attributed to the sensory part of human nature is its attraction to the immediacy of an event or experience. Once that immediacy has passed or no longer holds its attention, human nature looks elsewhere.

Thus, even "while a soul is with God in deep spiritual prayer, it will passively experience sensual rebellions, movements, and acts in the senses, not without its own great displeasure" (*ibid.*). Interestingly, Saint John tells us that "this frequently happens at the time of Communion. Since the soul receives joy and gladness in this act of love — for the Lord grants the grace and gives himself for this reason

— the sensory part also takes its share" (*ibid.*). We know by experience that we can have distractions and other disturbances that come from within us precisely when we assume that we will have a respite from them given the context in which we find ourselves; for example, when receiving Communion.

This is to be expected given the realities of human nature and the complexities of life. In the midst of all this, we must determine where we will direct our focus. We can follow the lead of our senses and focus on whatever is preoccupying us at the time. Even when our intention is to quiet that preoccupation, it can become yet more intense. Or, we can strive to maintain our focus on the Eucharistic Lord within us. There is no guarantee that our striving will be successful, but it will reflect the desire and direction of our will.

In our spiritual practices, including the Eucharist, John's advice is that we avoid carelessness which strives "more for spiritual savor than for spiritual purity and discretion" (*Dark Night*, I, 6:1). Otherwise we gradually become "more eager just to receive Communion than to receive it with a pure and perfect heart" (*ibid.*, 6:4). Such carelessness is a consequence of assigning priority to the delight we experience in our spiritual practices. Left unchallenged, such a priority will eventually redirect our will from our encounter with the Lord in the Eucharist to the delightful experiences we may associate with it.

John of the Cross summarizes his teaching as follows:

> In receiving Communion they spend all their time trying to get some feeling and satisfaction rather than humbly praising and reverencing God dwelling within them. And they go about this in such a way that, if they do not procure any sensible feeling and satisfaction, they think they have accomplished nothing. As a result they judge very poorly of God and fail to understand that the sensory benefits are the least among those that this most blessed Sacrament bestows, for the invisible grace it gives is a greater blessing. God often withdraws sensory delight and pleasure so that souls might set the eyes of faith on this invisible grace. (*ibid.*, 6:5)

Saint John calls us to approach the Eucharist, and indeed the entire spiritual journey, in such a way that we will see — and live — with "the eyes of faith."

"Come closer to the loved one"

The journey on which Saint John of the Cross leads us will guide us toward an ever-deepening union with God. As that union intensifies, so too does our willingness to embrace whatever the Lord may ask of us. We may not always understand precisely what the Lord is doing, and there is no guarantee that we will find it agreeable. Nevertheless, we embrace fully and willingly the Lord's presence and activity in our life because we believe them to be the means of our transformation. Our attentiveness to the Lord gradually unites our will with God's own. John teaches us that those who seek something other than God will neither appreciate nor be attracted to the Lord's words or ways or works.

This is the perspective with which he interprets Jesus' teaching on the Eucharist. When Jesus introduces this teaching to his followers, he identifies himself as the "bread of life." He promises that "whoever eats of this bread will live forever; and the bread that I will give for the life of the world is my flesh" (cf. John 6:48-51). As is often the case in response to Jesus' teachings, his disciples discuss and debate what his words could mean. Jesus explains further. "Those who eat my flesh and drink my blood have eternal life" (6:53). The reaction is less than welcoming; his words are too much for his listeners. "When many of his disciples heard it, they said, 'This teaching is difficult; who can accept it?'" (6:60). As the scene concludes, "many of his disciples turned back and no longer went about with him" (6:66).

In commenting on this gospel scene, Saint John of the Cross notes especially the motivation of the crowd which prompted them to look for Jesus on this occasion. Jesus himself identifies it when the crowd reaches him; "You are looking for me not because you saw signs but because you ate the loaves and were filled" (John 6:26). The contrast is sharp. Jesus wants to teach them of heavenly bread which leads to eternal life; they came expecting only earthly bread which perishes.

In his book which focuses on union with God, *Living Flame of Love*, John of the Cross summarizes the story in this way. "The loftier were the words of the Son of God, the more tasteless they were to the impure, as happened when he preached the sovereign and loving doctrine of the Holy Eucharist, for many turned away" (Stanza 1:5). Once again our will has a critical role in shaping the quality of our spiritual journey and especially our relationship with the Eucharist.

In sanjuanist spirituality, the will is made for love and, by love, for union with God. Our participation in the Eucharist, our reception of Communion, is a privileged moment in which we are strengthened by love itself for love and union. The Eucharist beckons us to become love, to become what we receive, to be transformed into the living likeness of the Lord Jesus. We must choose, we must decide that nothing will stand in the way of that transformation. In the commentary on his great love poem between Christ and the soul, *Spiritual Canticle*, John of the Cross says bluntly, "anyone truly in love will let all other things go in order to come closer to the loved one" (Stanza 29:10).

"Let all other things go." This is what must be done if we are to benefit fully from all that the Eucharist offers to us. This is what must be done if we sincerely want to cooperate with the grace of God that guides and sustains our spiritual journey. This is what must be done if we truly desire and choose "to come closer to the loved one."

"Receive Communion as usual"

Saint John of the Cross views the Eucharist primarily through the lens of the spiritual life. His language reflects his considerable skills as a theologian and a keen observer of human experiences within the spiritual journey. A casual reading of such language could make us hesitant in approaching the Eucharist; we might feel that our unworthiness prevents us from encountering the Lord in this way. Engendering any type of hesitation is far removed from John's intention; the Eucharist ever remains the "bread of life." It is necessary sustenance for the journey.

John of the Cross is a religious and a priest, a poet, a theologian, and a mystic. His vision of the spiritual life and his understanding of the Lord's presence and activity within the spiritual life are influenced by all those realities. However, John is also a pastor and a spiritual director. He offered guidance and direction to his Carmelite brothers and sisters as well as to many others from a wide range of lifestyles and occupations. He was always ready to listen to the life-experience of another and to respond with care and compassion, charity and challenge. John is a saint and a Doctor of the Church, not solely because of his enduring teaching and doctrine, but because he lived as Jesus lived, he loved as Jesus loved.

In terms of his writings, Saint John's pastoral abilities are most evident in his letters. Though not many of his letters have survived, those which have been preserved are testimonies to his practical and pastoral insight and advice regarding human nature and the spiritual life, and his wisdom in guiding others along the pathways toward union with God. These reflections will conclude with the wisdom from one of his letters.

Juana de Pedraza, of Granada, was among Saint John's regular correspondents, though only two of his letters to her have survived. None of her letters to him are extant. Almost nothing is known about this woman other than that John served as her confessor and director during the time he lived in Granada. The two surviving letters to her were written during the year after he moved from Granada to Segovia; they address issues which she must have discussed with John on earlier occasions.

Saint John writes to Juana in response to the "darkness and voids of spiritual poverty" she has been experiencing for some time (cf. Letter 19). She feels that everyone and everything have failed to support her, including God. John assures her that such experiences are consistent with growth in the spiritual life, so she should not make any adjustments to her spiritual practices, on her own, based upon those experiences. John encourages and challenges her, "you are making good progress. Do not worry, but be glad! Who are you that you should guide yourself? Wouldn't that end up fine!" (*ibid.*).

After explaining to her and reminding her that God is at work during those dark periods in the spiritual life, Saint John advises her regarding the appropriate way to respond:

> Walk along the level road of the law of God and of the Church, and live only in dark and true faith and certain hope and complete charity, expecting all our blessings in heaven.... Rejoice and trust in God, for he has given you signs that you can very well do so.... Desire no other path than this and adjust your soul to it (for it is a good one) and receive Communion as usual.... Should you have some problem, write to me about it. (*ibid.*)

"Receive Communion as usual." John calls us to fidelity whatever may be our spiritual experiences.

Our faithful participation in the Eucharist, our regular encounter with the Lord in Communion, reflect our will's desire and intention to be one with God. And that desire and intention are the foundations upon which God's work of transformation begins to unfold within us.

"Receive Communion as usual." In the Eucharist, "the soul receives joy and gladness" (*Dark Night*, I, 4:2). At times it may be a joy we do not sense and a gladness we do not perceive. Yet, we can be confident that the Lord is present and active within us, nourishing us, strengthening us, guiding us along the pathways to eternal life, to "joy and gladness."

"The Lifelong Banquet of God's Grace"

Saint Francis de Sales

The next person we meet brings us to another country and another century, seventeenth-century France. Imagine a personal resume that sounds as if it had been prepared by a candidate for multiple categories of "Who's Who": Aristocrat by birth and background, gifted student with excellent communication skills, trained as a civil and canon lawyer, able theologian and philosopher, insightful writer, exceptional spiritual director, priest, bishop, founder of a religious community. Our immediate reaction to such a list might be to assume that it describes more than one person if not a group of people. However, this is the personal resume of Francis de Sales. There is yet more for, even after his death, the list expanded with the addition of saint, Doctor of the Church, patron of spiritual directors. Saint Francis himself might have prepared a much shorter resume highlighting simply what he wanted to be and become throughout his life — a seeker of God and a lover of God, and that he would work tirelessly so those he served would desire and become the same.

Born in 1567, of the de Boisy family, in the Chateau de Sales, Francis grew up in a society and a historical period in which every component of his resume became an effective channel for the pastoral concern and care of the people he served. Francis was ever aware that, on his own, he could not accomplish all that the Lord called him to do. He knew the priority of his relationship with God and of participating in the life of the Body of Christ, the Church. He embraced that priority fully and he lived it in an exemplary way.

Saint Jane de Chantal, Francis' close friend and co-foundress with him of the Visitation Sisters, wrote in a letter that he would often teach the need

> to humble yourself profoundly under God's holy hand, to let yourself be led by way of His good pleasure and, following that same good pleasure, to offer no resistance to whatever He may wish to

> do with you and to correspond to His grace by fidelity to the opportunities presented to you by Providence. Our blessed Father valued beyond measure these practices and faithfully observed them. (To Noël Brulart, February, 1632)

Saint Francis' fidelity in corresponding to God's grace was nurtured and sustained by his involvement in the life of the Church and his regular reception of the sacraments. The Eucharist was a source of nourishment for him and he wrote of it eloquently. This chapter will explore some aspects of Saint Francis de Sales' perspective on "the blessed sacrament of the Eucharist, the lifelong banquet of God's grace" (*The Love of God*, Bk. 3, Ch. 11).

"God has become our very food"

As many others have done over the course of Church history, Saint Francis speaks of the Eucharist as food, as essential nourishment for our continued spiritual growth and development. In commenting on the Eucharist, most writers will highlight the benefits accessible to us through our regular reception of this food and nourishment. Francis, however, adopts a different perspective. He emphasizes the attitude and action of Jesus in providing us with this great gift:

> You cannot consider our Savior in an action more full of love or more tender than this. In it he abases himself, if we may so express it, and changes himself into food, so that he may penetrate our souls and unite himself most intimately to the heart and body of the faithful. (*Introduction to the Devout Life*, Part 2, Ch. 21)

This attitude of love and act of humility have but one goal: intimate union with us. This is the attitude and action of our God who longs for us and seeks to be one with us.

Such an attitude and action have been God's mode of operation since creation. Throughout salvation history, God has nurtured a love relationship with us. Maintaining this relationship demands a genuine mutuality:

> God is not unaware of our love for him, since it is his gift to us; nor can we be unaware of his love for us, since he has proclaimed it so widely; we also recognize that all good things we possess are due to his benevolence. (*The Love of God*, Bk. 2, Ch. 22)

The Eucharist is situated in the context of this mutual awareness; in fact, it represents a pinnacle in the relationship. As Saint Francis tells us, "To crown this loving relationship, God has become our very food in the blessed sacrament of the Eucharist" (*ibid.*). God's continuing presence among us through this sacrament is a permanent and powerful expression of God's union with us. It is also a constant and consistent reminder of God's longing for us; the Eucharist is a demonstration and a celebration of God's love.

There is an obvious communal dimension within this sacrament. It brings us together and sustains us as a faith community, the Body of Christ, the Church. Because this dimension is so prominent in our celebration of the Eucharist, it would be easy to assume that it sums up the nature of this sacrament. However, the Eucharist is intensely personal; it is not a generic gift that fails to recognize the significance and uniqueness of each person. Quite the contrary, it is a personal gift, an expression of God's love for us as individuals. That gift is an invitation to union:

> So that all people individually might be
> intimately united to his goodness — not

merely human nature as such — he instituted the sacrament of the holy Eucharist, which each can share and so achieve personal union with the Savior, in reality and by way of food. It is this sacramental union… which impels us towards and promotes union of soul with God. (*The Love of God*, Bk. 7, Ch. 2)

This personal dimension demands responsibility. We cannot remain passive when touched by such extravagant love. We must do whatever we can to welcome the invitation to union with God that the Eucharist extends to us. The Lord's love and humility make this sacrament possible; our response will be best expressed through reciprocity — our love for the Lord, our humble acknowledgment of dependence on God, and our desire for union with God. Such is the nourishment provided by this food.

"Advance, strengthen, and comfort yourself in the love of God"

From Saint Francis' perspective, maintaining the quality of our dispositions is among our primary responsibilities in receiving the Eucharist.

There is power in our dispositions, they are a gauge which determines the extent to which this sacrament will have a lasting impact on our life. Francis is writing during a time when the frequent reception of the Eucharist was rare for most people. Thus it was a significant event for which preparation was particularly important. Nevertheless, the qualities of life that Saint Francis identifies as preparation for receiving the Eucharist have a value that extends beyond his historical period.

"Go with great confidence and with great humility to receive this heavenly food which nourishes you for everlasting life" (*Introduction to the Devout Life*, Part 2, Ch. 21). Confidence and humility are basic dispositions in our approach to the Eucharist. Confidence expresses our trust and conviction regarding God's love for us. Simply because the Eucharist is a sacrament of love is no guarantee that we will always sense or perceive that love at work in our life. Sometimes we may experience little more than distance or even absence. Confidence, built on faith, challenges us to trust, to acknowledge, to embrace the truth that God is ever at work within and around us.

Humility is inseparable from such confidence, for it demonstrates our dependence on God in all things. Apart from this disposition we could become quite complacent about the necessity of the Eucharist for our spiritual life. If we do not see and accept our need for dependence on God, then we will fix our attention elsewhere for support in our spiritual life. Whatever or wherever that "elsewhere" may be will fall short of the graces extended to us in this sacrament.

With this confidence and humility, we can then approach the Eucharist "full of faith, hope, and charity, and receive him in whom, by whom, and for whom we believe, hope, and love" (*ibid.*). In this great sacrament, Jesus is the milieu, the means, and the meaning for our faith, hope, and love; it enables us to identify with Jesus. Our longing for such identification must be primary among our dispositions for it will facilitate our transformation into the living likeness of Jesus.

Saint Francis' instruction is clear: "Your great intention in receiving Communion should be to advance, strengthen, and comfort yourself in the love of God. You must receive with love that which love alone has caused to be given to you" (*ibid.*). The Eucharist is not automatic; we must intend to "advance," to progress in our love for God. We must intend to "strengthen" ourselves in that love, to develop the stamina for living faithfully the example of Jesus. And we must intend to "comfort" ourselves in God's love, especially when discouragement or disappointment envelops us. The power of our intention is that it can draw us ever deeper into the transforming grace of God's love. Even when we cannot receive the Eucharist, the importance of our intention remains a notable means for union with God. "When you cannot enjoy the benefit of communicating in reality at Holy Mass, go to Communion at least in heart and spirit by uniting yourself in ardent desire to the life-giving Body of the Savior" (*ibid.*). Such union, born of our longing for the Lord, is a grace for our spiritual life.

We live at a time when receiving the Eucharist is more frequent and common than in Francis' era; nevertheless, his advice to those who were regular recipients has a wisdom which spans the centuries:

> If worldly people ask you why you receive Communion so often, tell them that it is to learn to love God, be purified from your imperfections, delivered from misery, comforted in affliction, and supported in weakness.... Tell them that you receive the Blessed Sacrament often so as to learn how to receive it well, for we

hardly do an action well which we do not practice often. (*ibid.*)

This is a learning in which we can always advance so the blessings of the Eucharist will become increasingly evident in our daily life.

"Dedicate every moment of life to divine love"

Jesus himself articulated the fundamental blessing that we receive through the Eucharist, "Whoever eats of this bread will live forever" (John 6:51). This is the Lord's own promise to us, but it is also a challenge to take responsibility for the new and eternal life at work within us through this sacrament. Saint Francis provides us with a further insight into Jesus' promise. He notes that the Eucharist "so effectively builds up the soul's health that it is almost impossible to be poisoned by evil affection of any kind.... People can avoid spiritual death by virtue of this sacrament of life" (*Introduction to the Devout Life*, Part 2, Ch. 20). It is our responsibility to care for our health physically and spiritually; the alternatives are carelessness and foolish lack of concern for life itself. Jesus' promise is sure; nevertheless, we must accept the responsibility for nurturing the eternal life offered to us.

The Eucharist accomplishes its work within us through a gradual transformation. "By adoring and eating beauty, purity, and goodness itself in this divine sacrament you will become wholly beautiful, wholly good, and wholly pure" (*ibid.*, Part 2, Ch. 21). We become what we receive. This has important implications for our life, for the effect of our encounters with the Eucharist is not incidental; rather, it is incremental. There will be a real and identifiable progress which unfolds in our life. Very simply, we share in the life of the Lord and take on the Lord's own likeness.

There is a great joy in this, joy born of the conviction that "it is not flesh and blood, but the Father in heaven who has revealed to (us) that (our) Savior, body and soul, is really present within (our) own bodies and souls in this sacrament" (*The Love of God*, Bk. 6, Ch. 7). There is yet more. Saint Francis teaches us that we also "experience the awareness which faith gives of that divine seed of immortality — an awareness bringing to the soul a comfort, a refreshment past all belief" (*ibid.*).

Receiving the Eucharist cannot be careless and casual; our approach must be purposeful and practical. We must want the Lord's grace of transformation to unfold within us, and we must want to cooperate with that grace in any way possible. Saint Francis proposes a plan for us in this regard:

> After you have received him, excite your heart to do homage to the King of salvation. Converse with him concerning your inmost concerns. Reflect that he is within you and has come there for your happiness. In fine, make him as welcome as you possibly can and conduct yourself in such manner that by your actions all may know that God is with you. (*Introduction to the Devout Life*, Part 2, Ch. 21)

Francis identifies five tasks for responding to the graces of the Eucharist. First, "do homage." We must demonstrate the reverence and honor that celebrate the presence of the Lord within us. Second, "converse with him." However simple or sophisticated our articulation, we have a privileged opportunity to share with the Lord Jesus what is most important and valuable to us in life. Third, "reflect." Recognize and acknowledge that the Lord is present with us, for us. Fourth, "welcome." The Lord must find a home within us, a place that is made familiar and comfortable by our faith and love. Fifth, "conduct yourself." None of the preceding tasks will be effective unless the witness of our daily life makes it unambiguously evident that God is present and active in our life.

In cooperating with the graces which the Eucharist offers to us, we choose to live as Jesus lived, with the new life that he has promised to us. This is a choice we make in light of God's extravagant love:

> He made us his own by baptism; he has cared for us, soul and body, with a love that passes knowledge; to win life for us, he suffered death; his own body and blood have been our food. After that, we have no choice but to come to the only conclusion possible: that being alive should no longer mean living with our own life, but with his life who died for us. In other words, we are to dedicate every moment of life to the divine love that inspired our Savior's death; we are to deliver up all our prey — all our victories, our virtues, our activities, our thoughts, everything on which our hearts are set. (*The Love of God*, Bk. 7, Ch. 8)

Such dedication is to live as Jesus lived, it is to live the Eucharist.

"I never receive Communion without you"

The Eucharist is personal not private, individual not isolationist. Though this sacrament touches us on profound levels of our being, it does not separate us from other members of the Body of Christ. In fact, it has precisely the opposite effect; it draws us into union with others, and especially those with whom we share faith as followers of Jesus. Such unity must characterize the interactions among all those who belong to the Body of Christ. This is also a function of healthy self-knowledge. As we grow in knowledge of ourselves, and particularly as we grow in the awareness and acceptance of our need for God, we understand more clearly the support and encouragement that we can receive and offer through our relationships and union with others. We understand, too, that our union with them transcends physical proximity; it is by heart that we are united to one another.

For Saint Francis, the Eucharist was a privileged arena in which he was especially at one with those who were significant in his life. This sentiment is articulated briefly in several of his letters. He writes to Madame Brûlart, one of his many directees and a close friend of Saint Jane de Chantal,

"I beg you to remember me in your prayers and communions, and I assure you that I shall always remember you in mine" (3 May 1604). We are challenged to remember others as we pray and celebrate the Eucharist so they will be a part of our faith life, so we might be more firmly united with them in the Lord.

The Eucharistic union which Francis nurtured with his friends and associates is expressed most eloquently and directly in his correspondence with Saint Jane. "I never say holy Mass without you and all those closest to you; I never receive Communion without you, and finally, I am as much yours as you could ever wish me to be" (24 June 1604). Years later, after Francis' death, Jane writes in very similar terms to one of her directees. "To my knowledge, I don't think I ever fail to remember you, especially at holy communion, and I never want to fail in this" (to Noël Brulart, 1634).

The relationship between Saint Francis de Sales and Saint Jane de Chantal was personally enriching for both of them and distinctly beneficial for others. Their relationship had a genuine apostolic quality; together, they founded a religious community and influenced the lives of many others by supporting and guiding them to deepen their relationship with the Lord. Both were gifted spiritual directors and assisted one another in that gift. Their relationship was a source of mutual consolation and encouragement, a truly exemplary friendship. It is not surprising, then, that Francis writes to Jane, "It is a special comfort for me on feast days to know that we go to communion together" (14 October 1604).

We, too, can find such comfort in knowing that we are one, through the Eucharist, with those who are a part of our life. And even more, we thereby deepen and strengthen that union, enabling us — indeed, commissioning us — to nurture unity of hearts among others. This will be a significant contribution to the transformation of our world.

"This gift of himself now is a reality"

Associated with the Eucharist throughout Church history have been profound promises, sublime language, and resplendent blessings. There is no surprise here; Jesus himself refers to the Eucharist as "bread from heaven," "living bread." His promise is unambiguous: "Whoever eats this bread will live forever" (John 6:58). Saint Francis de Sales' contribution to Eucharistic spirituality is no exception to that wealth of promises and language and blessings. His writings reflect the awe and majesty of this sacrament as well as the scope and seriousness of the responsibility we bear to live the effects of the Eucharist in our daily life.

We limit that responsibility if we conveniently relegate the personal implications of the Eucharist to some future point. Everyday life, then, would become merely a period of waiting for some moment that is yet to dawn upon us. And, in the waiting, we could become somewhat lethargic about responding to the graces of transformation offered to us. Francis reminds us that the gifts of this sacrament are present to us now; we must respond now:

> Unlimited happiness! — and not merely held out to us in the future; we have an earnest of it in the blessed sacrament of the Eucharist, the lifelong banquet of God's grace. There we receive the Savior's body and blood: his blood given us through his flesh; his substance offered to us substantially in a physical way, to teach us that he is to share his essence with us in this way at the eternal wedding-feast of glory. Undoubtedly this gift of himself now is a reality, though hidden under the appearance and likeness

of bread; but in heaven God will give himself to us unveiled. (*The Love of God*, Bk. 3, Ch. 11)

The Lord's self-gift to us now is precisely the foundation for Saint Francis' wonderful description of the Eucharist as the "lifelong banquet of God's grace." The banquet is now and we have been invited. The fact that "in heaven God will give himself to us unveiled" is a tremendous support for our hope and our trust in God's promises. But that hope and trust do not diminish the truth that "the gift of himself now is a reality"; a reality to be pondered frequently, a reality for which to be grateful, a reality that is instrumental in our transformation.

Saint Francis de Sales assures us today, as he has done through his writings for countless others over four hundred years, "the principal means of uniting yourself to God are the sacraments and prayer" (to Madame Brûlart, 3 May 1604). These means are accessible to us and we should frequently tap the transforming power within them. They are for our growth and development as followers of Jesus. They remind us that we need not rely solely on our own resources for building and nurturing our relationship with the Lord; in fact, it would be imprudent to do so with such graced means at our disposal.

Our relationship with the Lord must be a priority in life; we "renew that relationship by receiving the Redeemer's body in the blessed sacrament of the holy Eucharist" (*The Love of God*, Bk. 3, Ch. 8). Our fidelity to this relationship and our integrity in living it demonstrate our desire for union with God and confirm our love for God. Such is the Eucharistic quality of life, the "lifelong banquet," to which Saint Francis de Sales calls us.

"The Greatest Gift His Love Could Give"

SAINT ALPHONSUS DE LIGUORI

Now we return to Italy, but we move forward from the fourteenth century of Saint Catherine of Siena to the eighteenth century. Any exploration of the Church's moral teaching and the principles and practices of the ascetical life will lead us eventually to the wisdom and teaching of Saint Alphonsus de Liguori. So significant is his contribution to the development of moral, ascetical, and devotional theology that it would be possible to overlook the full richness of the many other gifts and talents that marked his life and ministry.

Born in the kingdom of Naples, four years before the beginning of the eighteenth century, in 1696, he was baptized Alphonsus Mary Anthony John Francis Cosmas Damian Michael Caspar de

Liguori, reflecting the Italian custom of naming a baby in honor of the family's favorite saints and patrons. He was born into a world of class consciousness; a world in which the quality of one's education and the caliber of one's riding and fencing skills were gauges of a good upbringing and sure blueprints for a successful and prosperous future. Alphonsus excelled at all these, and more.

Having completed his studies in civil and canon law at an unusually early age, Alphonsus was expected to get married and settle into a lucrative career as a lawyer. However, the loss of an important legal case, resulting from a relatively simple oversight on his part, drove him to abandon the practice of law and consider a vocation in the Church. He had pondered the possibility of a vocation to the priesthood a few years earlier but, in view of his father's vigorous opposition, he remained in the legal profession. After the humiliation of losing the court case, however, his desire and determination to redesign his future solidified.

Saint Alphonsus' decision to seek priestly ordination involved a painful journey that placed him at odds with his family and particularly with his father. Though Don Giuseppe de Liguori did eventually consent to his son's ecclesiastical career, it was not without a difficult and extended confrontation that Alphonsus remembered for the rest of his life.

The professional and personal pain of those early years did not dim the bright accomplishments of Saint Alphonsus' life of ninety-one years. During that long life he served as a priest, missionary, founder of the Congregation of the Most Holy Redeemer (Redemptorists), and diocesan bishop. In addition, he was a prolific writer on the important theological, moral, and doctrinal issues of his day, an accomplished musician and composer, a painter, and a pastoral, compassionate, and much sought-after confessor and spiritual director. Completing this brief portrait are his death in 1787, canonization in 1839, declaration as a Doctor of the Church in 1871, and designation as patron of confessors and moral theologians in 1950.

These present reflections will examine some insights which Saint Alphonsus de Liguori offers to us concerning the "sacrament of love," the Eucharist, to which he had a particular devotion throughout his life.

"Totally one with us"

As so many others had done in the centuries before him, and would do in the centuries following, Saint Alphonsus understood the Eucharist as food which nourishes our spiritual life and nurtures our relationship with the Lord. This aspect of the Eucharist is very practical for Alphonsus; as food, Jesus unites himself to us physically and spiritually. It is an intimate union with the Lord. "Jesus Christ's giving himself to us as food was the ultimate degree of love, for he gives himself to us to become totally one with us just as food becomes one with the person who eats it" (*The Practice of the Love of Jesus Christ*, 2:9). We must make the effort to receive Communion, but the resulting unity is Jesus' initiative. This is no superficial encounter; Jesus chooses to be "totally one" with us, facilitating and furthering our transformation into his likeness.

"He wished to give us his body, once sacrificed for us on the Cross, as our food so that through it, he could become united to each one of us" (*ibid.*, 3:7). Through our participation in and reception of the Eucharist, we are united with the crucified and risen Lord. The cross and resurrection — the entirety of the Paschal Mystery — will be the key elements in our transformation. For Saint Alphonsus, there is an inseparable relationship between the Eucharist and the Lord's Passion: both are profound expressions of God's love. The Eucharist does not spare us from experiencing the Paschal Mystery; quite the contrary, it situates us at the foot of the cross, but also at the entrance of the empty tomb. In the Eucharist we learn that these realities must unfold in our life also.

Very affirming for our spiritual life is the truth that Jesus wants to be with us in the Eucharist. It is not a haphazard decision on the Lord's part. In coming to us specifically as food, Jesus presents himself as accessible and available:

> Jesus desires very much to come to us in Holy Communion.… He left himself to us under the appearance of bread so that everyone might be able to receive him. If he had left himself under the appearance of some rare or costly food, the poor would not have been able to receive him. But he left himself under the appearance of bread, which is cheap and is available to everyone, so that people in every land could find him and receive him. (*Ibid.*, 2:5)

There is a universality, a catholicity, within this perspective; all have access to Jesus as this food. An important challenge for the Christian community is to assure that neither social status nor economic privilege become a criterion for union with the Lord through the Eucharist. Jesus welcomes all people; he wants to be encountered, to be accessible and available in the Eucharist because he desires and chooses to be with us.

Jesus comes to us as food that we might possess him completely. Love alone enables such vulnerability:

> God's great love has so arranged things that he gives himself to us not just in the eternal kingdom, but even here below he allows us to possess him in the greatest intimacy possible, by giving himself to us under the appearance of bread in this sacrament.... Until such time as we come to our homeland, Jesus wishes to give himself to us and to remain completely united to us. (*Ibid.*, 2:7)

Saint Alphonsus thus identifies the very heart of Jesus' motive in giving himself to us in the Eucharist.

"Love alone led Jesus to give us himself"

Jesus institutes the Eucharist in the context of a sacred meal with his disciples, a final meal during which he demonstrates the priority of love and service as the principal expressions of following his example, continuing his mission, and preaching his message. He is near the end of his life and, as Saint John tells us, he "knew that his hour had come" (13:1). What transpires during this meal, then, is particularly significant. Saint Alphonsus writes, "Knowing that the time had come for him to leave this earth and that he was soon to die for us, our loving Savior wished to leave us the greatest gift his love could give, the gift of the most holy sacrament" (*The Practice of the Love of Jesus Christ*, 2:1).

The "greatest gift." Among all the gifts that Jesus had already given through his life and preaching and healing and teaching, Alphonsus ranks this gift as the greatest. Through it Jesus gives to us, in a complete and lasting way, his very self. Even before his death and resurrection, Jesus places himself completely at our disposal. He gives us his life. Through the Eucharist and the entirety of the Paschal Mystery, Jesus demonstrates an incomparable love. Saint Alphonsus explains further that the

Eucharist holds within itself every other gift we have received from God:

> This sacrament was rightly called by St. Thomas Aquinas "the sacrament and the pledge of love." It is a "sacrament of love" because it was love alone which led Jesus to give us himself completely in it; it is a "pledge of love," so that if we were ever to doubt his love, we might have proof of it in this sacrament.... It contains every other gift the Lord has given us — creation, redemption, the call to glory. The Eucharist is not alone the pledge of Christ's love; it is also a pledge that he wishes to give us paradise. (*Ibid.*, 2:3)

Such an affirmation can be of tremendous support for our spiritual life. Along the pathways of our spiritual journey we will experience times of dryness and doubt, times when we question whether God is still present and active in our life, times of wondering if God cares for us and for our world. It is precisely then that the Eucharist reminds us of God's love throughout salvation history, of all that Jesus has done and continues to do for us. Even more it is a promise of the new life yet to come and of a share in God's reign. "The great love of Jesus Christ has conceived and brought about what human beings could not imagine or even believe.… This is no earthly food, it is I giving myself to you" (*ibid.*, 2:4).

For Jesus, love is the motive and the means of all he does. Through love, Jesus gives us himself in the Eucharist; by love, he longs to be with us; in love, he remains with us. The Eucharist reflects Jesus' desire to build an intimate relationship with us. For Saint Alphonsus, such a love goes beyond understanding:

> Love makes us wish to be in the presence of the one we love. It is this love which makes Jesus Christ remain with us in the Blessed Sacrament.… There is one thing I cannot comprehend and that is how God could love us to such an extent as to become bread for us. This love is a truth of faith totally beyond my comprehension. O love of Jesus, make yourself known to us and loved in return! (*Novena to the Sacred Heart*, Second Meditation)

The challenge of Jesus' love for us is not to understand it, but to accept it. Jesus remains present among us in the Eucharist "with apparently no other purpose than to demonstrate his love for us all" (*ibid.*). Do we believe this? Are we willing to allow this truth of our faith to sustain us on the journey? Will we embrace God's immeasurable love for us? Will we choose to live the consequences of that love in our daily life?

"It does not simply depend on feelings"

Our responses to those questions require faith. Regardless of what we may feel or sense about a particular point in our spiritual life, only faith will enable us to accept the immensity of the gift that is offered to us in the Eucharist. Our feelings are part of our spiritual journey because they are part of human nature. We must determine what weight we will accord them. Nevertheless, they do not serve well as accurate gauges for our progress nor as definite indicators for determining the nature and extent of God's work in our life. Faith facilitates our progress; faith gives us the vision to see God at work; faith accepts the union with Jesus to which we are invited in the Eucharist. As Saint Alphonsus writes, "In Holy Communion, Jesus unites himself to the soul and the soul is united to Jesus. It does not simply depend on feelings, for it is a true and real union" (*The Practice of the Love of Jesus Christ*, 2:8). Such union does not depend on feelings because it cannot; this union takes place deep within our spirit where only faith has eyes to see.

Alphonsus lived during that long period in Church history when receiving the Eucharist was infrequent and, sometimes, even rare in a person's life. Feelings of unworthiness abounded and, to some degree, were fostered. The willingness to receive Communion was practically equated with feelings of worthiness and sinlessness. If such feelings were not present, then it was assumed that regular reception would be frowned upon. Liturgy was marked more by pageant than participation. It became the custom, then, for people to ask their confessor or spiritual director for permission to receive Communion. Saint Alphonsus cautions his readers not to make the request for such permission contingent upon the presence of certain feelings:

> As regards the reception of Holy Communion, obey your spiritual director and even if you do not experience sensible devotion do not omit to ask permission to receive Holy Communion. Spiritual

directors are accustomed to grant permission for reception of Holy Communion according to the eagerness which their
penitents manifest. When your director
sees that you do not request permission
to receive and that you show little eagerness in the matter, he will not ordinarily
instruct you to receive Holy Communion. (*Motives for Confidence in the Divine
Mercy*, 20)

Precisely because confessors and spiritual directors were accorded such authority in eighteenth-
century Italy, Alphonsus alerts them to sound
Church teaching regarding the place of feelings in
determining a person's eligibility for receiving the
Eucharist. After citing some instances when a spiritual director might refuse permission for the person to receive Communion, he writes:

At the same time it is important to note
even though St. Thomas insists that one
should approach Holy Communion with
great devotion, it is not necessary that
this devotion should be either of the highest degree or experienced in the external senses. It is sufficient if the director
discerns in his penitent a readiness to carry

out what the Lord wants. Souls who stay away from Holy Communion because they do not experience in themselves a great degree of sensible devotion resemble... those who feel the cold yet refuse to approach the heat because they do not experience in themselves any sense of warmth! (*Direction of Souls Who Wish to Lead a Deeply Spiritual Life*, 4:35)

The twenty-first century is, of course, a very different period in Church history and it might be easy to dismiss the teachings of Saint Alphonsus as relics of past times. However, the principles within his teachings have a timeless quality because they reflect the fundamental truths of Christianity and sound Eucharistic theology. Though we are not familiar today with the need to request permission before receiving Communion, the power of feelings in the spiritual life remains as evident today as it was more than two and a half centuries ago. Those fundamental truths remain the same. Alphonsus teaches us that it is not "necessary in order to continue one's practice of frequent Communion that the soul should be aware of or be able to feel spiritual progress since the spiritual effects of this sacrament are not always easily discernible" (*ibid.*). In fact, very little about our spiritual progress is "easily" discernible; nevertheless, the Eucharist does have an impact on our spiritual life. It remains for us to determine the best way to welcome and nurture that impact and so support our continued growth for the spiritual journey.

"Have a great desire"

"It is the experience of all those who exercise the ministry of spiritual direction, myself included, that those who approach Holy Communion with correct dispositions make considerable progress in their spiritual lives" (*Direction of Souls Who Wish to Lead a Deeply Spiritual Life*, 4:36). Though Saint Alphonsus does not provide us with a lengthy and invariable list of what he considers to be "correct dispositions," he does articulate some fundamental points that span the centuries and remain valuable for us today:

> We should be convinced that no one can do, nor even conceive of doing, anything more pleasing to Jesus Christ than of communicating with the dispositions appropriate to the great guest they are

to receive. I say "with the dispositions appropriate," not "in a worthy state," for if it were a matter of being worthy, who would ever be able to communicate? Only another God would be worthy to receive God. I mean "appropriate" insofar as that is possible for a poor creature clothed with the frail flesh of Adam. It is enough that a person, ordinarily speaking, receive in the state of grace and with a lively desire to grow in the love of Jesus Christ. (*The Practice of the Love of Jesus Christ*, 2:10)

These words reflect well Alphonsus' pastoral approach. He lived at a time during which the standards set for receiving Communion were so high that most people encountered their Eucharistic Lord only infrequently. Alphonsus shifts the base of those standards from worthiness to appropriateness, thus encouraging a frequency marked by regularity rather than restriction.

Appropriate dispositions for this Doctor of the Church include being in the state of grace and having a desire to grow in our love for the Lord. These two are related, for our responsiveness to grace fosters our desire to love. "We are talking about souls who have freed themselves from their deliberate attachment to venial sins, who have striven to overcome their sinful inclinations and have a great desire of approaching Holy Communion" (*Direction of Souls Who Wish to Lead a Deeply Spiritual Life*, 4:30). Striving to overcome sin and desiring the Eucharist are elaborations of the preceding two dispositions. An unaddressed inclination to sin is inconsistent with a serious and sincere response to grace; our desire for the Eucharist expresses a love for the Lord that ever seeks to be one with him.

Central to these dispositions is the emphasis that Saint Alphonsus gives to desire. If desire for the Eucharist is not a fixture in our spiritual life, we can compromise our love for the Lord and so too our continued progress. The desire of which Alphonsus speaks is no mere wish; it evolves into an act of the will, a way of being and behaving that influences every dimension of our life. The strength of that desire is rooted in our faith, in our conviction that Jesus is truly and fully present in the Eucharist and at work in our life. "Even though we cannot see him in the Eucharist, he sees us and is really present there. He is present so that we can possess him, but hidden in order that we might desire him" (*The Practice of the Love of Jesus Christ*, 2:7).

The fact that Jesus is hidden invites a desire born of faith. Without faith, our response to such hiddenness can degenerate into a discouragement and even despair which urge us to accept that this is no more than bread and wine, and that God no longer cares for us.

The ultimate disposition for approaching the Eucharist is that love which constitutes the very heart of the gospel itself. For Saint Alphonsus, "the two great mysteries of hope and love are the Passion of Jesus Christ and the Sacrament of the Altar" (*ibid.*, 3:7). It is by love that we unite ourselves with all that Jesus accomplished in the Paschal Mystery; it is by love that we are one with Jesus in the Eucharist. Our love is the only response worthy of Jesus' love for us. These two mysteries, reflecting the full depth and richness of Jesus' example to us, are the axes around which our spiritual life must be centered, for within them are the graces necessary for our transformation into the Lord's likeness. Alphonsus teaches us:

> Your love should be centered above all else on the two great mysteries of Our Lord's love, the Holy Sacrament of the Altar and the Passion of Jesus Christ. If the love of all human hearts could be

concentrated in one heart it would not
approach in the slightest degree to the
greatness of the love which Jesus Christ
has shown us in these two mysteries.
(*Motives for Confidence in the Divine
Mercy*, 21)

The challenge ever before us is to strive for the same
great love that Jesus has demonstrated for us by his
life and death, and by the gift of himself in the
Eucharist.

"We might become the same thing as he is"

In eighteenth-century Italy not every perspective on the Eucharist was helpful for continued
growth in the spiritual life. Some extremists taught
that almost perfect sinlessness was necessary to be
truly worthy of receiving Communion. Those who
were more moderate assumed that a substantial level
of spiritual maturity was required, thus making reception a privilege reserved for the elite. Even those
promoting a more flexible approach insisted that
Communion could never be received unless it was
preceded by the sacrament of Reconciliation. By
contrast, Saint Alphonsus believed and taught that

general accessibility was an important benefit in itself because "Communion was instituted also for the imperfect who are restored to health by means of this heavenly food" (*Direction of Souls Who Wish to Lead a Deeply Spiritual Life*, 4:33). This perspective clearly echoes Jesus' own, "Those who are well have no need for a physician, but those who are sick. I have come to call not the righteous but sinners to repentance" (Luke 5:31).

The pastoral sensitivity evident in the Liguorian perspective is not to be interpreted as condoning passivity on our part. The impact of the Eucharist on our spiritual life is not automatic; openness to the benefits of the Eucharist requires cooperation with grace and fidelity to the disciplines of our spiritual life. The alternative exposes us to a gradual deterioration and eventual devaluation of the spiritual journey itself:

> You should be careful about deliberate faults, if only because on their account God withholds light and help, and withdraws spiritual consolation from us. That is why some people find their spiritual duties wearisome and painful, and grow slack about prayer, Communion, visits

> to the Blessed Sacrament, novenas, and
> sometimes, unfortunately, even give up
> everything. (*The Practice of the Love of Jesus
> Christ*, 8:5)

Human weakness and sinfulness do not excuse us from being aware of and responsible for their influence on our spiritual life. Grace provides us with the possibility of overcoming "deliberate faults" and their influence, but we must take the initiative in responding to that grace.

Taking initiative does not mean that we rely solely on our own resources. Alphonsus was well aware that personal resources can be overtaxed and quickly drained leaving us with little more than feeling unworthy and powerless to respond. "Those pusillanimous souls who on account of an exaggerated sense of their unworthiness neglect to receive Holy Communion are thereby inflicting considerable harm to their own spiritual progress" (*Direction of Souls Who Wish to Lead a Deeply Spiritual Life*, 4:35). While we must use the resources we do have, we must also support our efforts with determination, prayer, and the sacramental life of the Church. Alphonsus' advice for those times when we are stalled is as valuable today as it was more than two centuries ago. "There are five remedies for tepidity, which enable us to resume the journey to perfection once more: (1) the desire for perfection; (2) the resolution to attain it; (3) mental prayer; (4) frequent Communion; (5) prayer" (*The Practice of the Love of Jesus Christ*, 8:8). In speaking to confessors and spiritual directors, he instructs them to be

> particularly attentive to their penitents when they experience aridity or spiritual desolation.... The confessor should be very diligent in these circumstances to encourage his penitents to persevere in prayer and above all not to omit to receive Holy Communion. (*Direction of Souls Who Wish to Lead a Deeply Spiritual Life*, 1:5)

Saint Alphonsus consistently highlights both the importance of the Eucharist and the frequent reception of it as priority supports for our spiritual life.

Our relationship to Jesus in the Eucharist draws us toward transformation. The goal of the spiritual life, and even of all the disciplines within it, is to live and love as Jesus lived and loved. The Incarnation and Redemption, indeed all of salvation history, encourage us and guide us in reaching that goal. "It was out of his great love for us that Jesus Christ wished to unite himself to us so much in order that we might become the same thing as he is" (*The Practice of the Love of Jesus Christ*, 2:8). Similarly, it must be out of our great love for the Lord Jesus that we seek and strive to be as he is.

"On no account omit to receive Communion"

Saint Alphonsus de Liguori promoted the frequent reception of Communion during a very tense time in Church history. The influence of Jansenism had infiltrated many aspects of ecclesial and civil life. Specifically in terms of the Eucharist was the insistence that reception should be rare, with some asserting that this rarity did not extend very much beyond once in a lifetime. For Alphonsus, such a restriction jeopardizes progress in the spiritual life by hindering the person from receiving the gift through which Jesus himself can be of direct support for the spiritual journey. His instructions to confessors and spiritual directors are eminently pastoral:

> When a soul commits some light fault and has not the opportunity of confessing, that person should on no account omit to receive Holy Communion.... I cannot see how any pastor could, without compelling reasons, conscientiously deny the reception of Holy Communion to those who request it.... It is certainly advisable, occasionally, to admit to Holy Communion those who are in danger of falling into mortal sins so that they might gain strength to avoid them. (*Direction of Souls Who Wish to Lead a Deeply Spiritual Life*, 4:28-29)

For this Doctor of the Church, rare should be the times when we do not receive the Eucharist. So strong is this conviction that he is compelled to recommend, "Even when you do not receive Communion sacramentally do so spiritually many times during the day" (*Motives for Confidence in the Divine Mercy*, 20).

Saint Alphonsus helped to promote and preserve an understanding of the Eucharist and a comfortability and regularity in approaching it that we accept as common practice in the twenty-first century. He would have acknowledged and applauded the Second Vatican Council's teaching and description of the Eucharist as "the source and summit of the Christian life" (*Dogmatic Constitution on the Church*, 2:11). We need to tap that source regularly for stamina on our journey to the summit.

The Eucharist is an intimate encounter with a person we love, a person who is the source and summit of our spiritual life, a person we want to please by our love. The Eucharist is well suited for such a personal relationship for, as Alphonsus reminds us, "a person can give no greater pleasure to Jesus Christ than receiving him frequently in the Sacrament of the Altar" (*The Practice of the Love of Jesus Christ*, 8:26). Truly, no greater pleasure can be given, because in this encounter with the Lord Jesus we receive "the greatest gift his love could give" (*ibid.*, 2:1).

"I Felt That I Was Loved"

In meeting the most recent and third woman Doctor of the Church, we return to France, though we must situate ourselves two hundred years after the life and work of Saint Francis de Sales. The popularity of this Discalced Carmelite religious, Saint Thérèse of Lisieux, has been consistent and widespread since her death in the late nineteenth century. Thérèse Martin was born in 1873 and, even though she lived for only twenty-four years, she provides us with an example and a teaching that have appealed to and inspired countless individuals in every culture and religious tradition.

Like the great foundress and founder of her religious community, Saints Teresa of Avila and John of the Cross, Saint Thérèse has a perspective on the Eucharist. That perspective is fashioned by the place of the Eucharist in her life and her intimate relationship with the Lord, her passionate desire for holiness and her doctrine of the Little Way, her apostolic spirit and her concern for the salvation of others. It emerged from within her life as she experienced everyday events. Reflecting on her First Communion, Thérèse writes, "I felt that I was loved" (*Story of a Soul*, IV). For her, it was a tangible experience of love, a love that would guide her life and define her vocation, a love in which she wanted others to have a share.

Saint Thérèse of Lisieux does not write about the Eucharist in any systematic way; she is not a trained theologian, nor is she educated much beyond what her family, a few years at boarding school, and a private tutor provided before her entrance into Carmel at age fifteen. Nevertheless, the Spirit was at work within her, giving her wisdom and insight beyond many of her superiors, elders, and peers. Within her reflections on the Eucharist, several areas of significance emerge, areas which can support our own relationship with the Lord Jesus.

"Hurry, give me the blessed bread"

The seeds of Saint Thérèse' desire for the Eucharist and her understanding of it are planted early in her family life. She tells a story from the time when she was four years old. During that era in French parishes, there was a custom of distributing bread that had been presented and blessed during Mass. Typically, this bread was used at the family's main meal on Sunday. Thérèse very much looked forward to eating some of this bread when her family returned from church:

> On Sunday, as I was too little to go to services, Mama stayed with me; I was very good, walking around on tiptoe during the Mass; but as soon as I saw the door open, there was an explosion of joy! I would throw myself in front of my pretty little sister… and say: "Oh, little Céline, hurry, give me the blessed bread!" (*Story*, I)

On those occasions when her family had been late for the distribution and was unable to receive the bread, her sister created the adaptation of praying the Hail Mary over a freshly cut slice of bread. Then, Thérèse relates, "After making a sign of the Cross

I would eat it with great devotion, finding it tasted the same as the blessed bread" (*ibid.*). She refers to this simple ritual as "my Mass." Even at this early stage in her life, Thérèse demonstrated the precociousness and boldness that would characterize her entire though brief life.

Her desire for and understanding of the Eucharist were further nurtured by daily walks with her father, which included a visit to the Blessed Sacrament, and by her participation in religious feasts:

> I loved above all the processions in honor
> of the Blessed Sacrament. What a joy it
> was for me to throw flowers beneath the
> feet of God! Before allowing them to fall
> to the ground, I threw them as high as
> I could and I was never so happy as when
> I saw my roses touch the sacred monstrance. (*Story*, II)

Through these childhood events, Thérèse gradually built a familiar and intimate relationship with her Eucharistic Lord. As this relationship developed, her desire for perfection intensified:

> One evening, I heard you (her older sister
> Pauline) say that from the time one re-

ceived one's First Communion, one had
to commence living a new life, and I
immediately made the resolution not to
wait for that day but to commence the
very same time as Céline. (*Story*, III)

All these events could be set aside as nothing more than a child's initial experiences of and
fascination with Church ceremony and particularly
the Eucharist. And yet, Saint Thérèse gives us a
valuable lesson in self-knowledge as she reflects on
the roots of her own love for the Eucharist. What
are my first memories of encountering the Eucharist?
How do those first encounters influence my relationship with the Eucharist even today? In which
ways have my relationship to the Lord and my
understanding of the Eucharist matured? These and
similar questions can help us to explore our own
Eucharistic roots. Such exploration is not merely
an exercise in nostalgia; rather, it can be a valuable
means for seeing the journey on which the Lord
has led us thus far, and of refreshing our desire for
the new life to which the Eucharist constantly invites us. The challenge is to continue the journey
and to accept the invitation.

"I could not have been better disposed"

Saint Thérèse writes of her First Communion as a pivotal moment in her life. Her family was very much involved in her preparation for that event; and, from her perspective, their efforts were effective. "The time of my First Communion remains engraved in my heart as a memory without any clouds. It seems to me I could not have been better disposed to receive Him than I was" (*Story*, IV). She writes about a small book of practices and devotions that her sister, Pauline, had made for her as part of the preparation. "It aided me in preparing my heart through a sustained and thorough method. Although I had already prepared it for a long time, my heart needed a new thrust" (*ibid.*). This is typical of Thérèse, always wanting to do more as far as the quality of her spiritual life was concerned.

After the three months of preparation, she makes a retreat with the other children who would receive the sacrament. Then, "the beautiful day of days finally arrived. The smallest details of that heavenly day have left unspeakable memories in my soul!" (*ibid.*). Yet she does speak about that day and her language reveals the depth and development of her relationship with the Lord:

How sweet was that first kiss of Jesus!
It was a kiss of love: I felt that I was loved,
and I said: "I love You, and I give myself to You forever!" There were no demands made, no struggles, no sacrifices;
for a long time now Jesus and poor little
Thérèse looked at and understood each
other. That day, it was no longer simply a look, it was a fusion; they were no
longer two. Thérèse had vanished as a
drop of water in the immensity of the
ocean. Jesus alone remained; He was the
Master, the King. (*ibid.*)

Saint Thérèse interprets this event as a loving and
transforming union. She experienced an intimacy
and union with the Lord that not only remained
with her throughout life, but intensified. She is
writing of this experience about twelve years after
it took place, after much more had unfolded in her
life; even then, she describes it as a complete giving of herself to the Lord. Indeed, she could not
have been better disposed.

Because frequent Communion was not a usual
practice in her day, a month passes before Thérèse
next receives the sacrament. She writes of that event
in similar terms. "I repeated to myself these words

of St. Paul: 'It is no longer I that live, it is Jesus who lives in me!' Since that Communion, my desire to receive grew more and more, and I obtained permission to go to Holy Communion on all the principal feasts" (*ibid.*). We live in a privileged time when it is possible to receive Communion regularly, even on a daily basis, and we are encouraged to do so. Thus it may strike us as odd to glimpse back at a time when permission to receive Communion was needed at all, not to mention on major feasts. Our experience of the Eucharist probably will not parallel that of Thérèse precisely because receiving Communion is more commonplace for us. However, her reflections teach us a fundamental truth about the Lord's work within us through this great gift.

By our encounters with the Eucharistic Lord we open ourselves to God's transforming work; it facilitates that "fusion" of which Saint Thérèse writes. This loving and transforming union will gradually refashion us, even as it did Thérèse, into the living likeness of the Lord. Through the Eucharist we are transformed by the sacred gift we consume; truly, it is the Lord who is then present and active in us and through us. We cooperate with all this to the degree that we are disposed to invite and welcome Jesus deep within our hearts. With Thérèse, we can pray: "My Beloved, come live in me. Oh! come, your beauty has ravished me. Deign to transform me into You!" (*Poetry*, PN25).

"Jesus will be so pleased in my heart"

For Saint Thérèse, the Eucharist cannot be summed up by our desires for union with the Lord; for the Lord, too, desires to be one with us. In Thérèsian spirituality, God's desire for union with us, God's longing to be close to us, is the basic reason for the gift of the Eucharist:

> It is not to remain in a golden ciborium that He comes to us each day from heaven; it's to find another heaven, infinitely more dear to Him than the first: the heaven of our soul, made to His image, the living temple of the adorable Trinity! (*Story*, V)

Thérèse understands well the truth that we are created in God's image and likeness, that we are good and beautiful, that we are endowed with a dignity which reflects God's creative handiwork within us. God seeks to be with us as with one that is dearly cherished and truly loved.

In writing to her sister, Pauline, thanking her for the small book used in preparing for First Communion, Thérèse says, "I desire, in fact, … that little Jesus will be so pleased in my heart that He will not think of going back to heaven" (*Letters*, I, LT11). That she could imagine Jesus being so pleased that he would not think of returning to heaven highlights Saint Thérèse' understanding and insight into the capacity of human nature to be a worthy dwelling place for God. Several years later, she refers to the soul as "a loved tabernacle" (*ibid.*, LT92). And in her "Act of Oblation to Merciful Love," she prays, "Remain in me as in a tabernacle and never separate Yourself from Your little victim" (*Story*, Appendix).

That Jesus desires to be with us is at the heart of Thérèsian spirituality of the Eucharist. Even as we are seeking union with the Lord through this sacrament, so Jesus is seeking to be with us there also. By our creation, because we reflect God's image and likeness, Jesus recognizes within us familiar territory for a dwelling place. So familiar is the heaven of our soul for Jesus, that Thérèse insists it is "infinitely more dear" to the Lord than the first heaven. Do we believe this of ourselves? Do we acknowledge and accept our own goodness as persons? We can allow many things and events in our world to tell us otherwise. And yet our faith urges us to believe that even as Jesus became like us through the Incarnation, so we become like Jesus through the Eucharist.

All this reflects Thérèsian anthropology. Her perspective on humanity in light of the Eucharist challenges us to embrace the truth that we are the Lord's preferred dwelling place. We reflect God and have the capacity for God, by creation. By our participation in the Eucharist we celebrate and reaffirm that truth, we proclaim our commitment to seek union with the Lord, and we become a living invitation for the Lord to remain with us. We must believe that our hearts will be pleasing to the Lord and that the Lord desires to remain within us. Our experience in this could very well reflect Thérèse' own, "He comes within me; by his presence I am a living Monstrance!" (*Poetry*, PN25).

"I will offer my Communion for you"

Saint Thérèse had an apostolic spirit, by heart she desired to love the entire world. Her life and most especially her health were such that she never had the opportunity to become a missionary. Still, the desire was deep and expansive within her. She writes:

> One mission alone would not be sufficient for me, I would want to preach the Gospel on all the five continents simultaneously and even to the most remote isles. I would be a missionary, not for a few years only but from the beginning of creation until the consummation of the ages. (*Story,* IX)

At one point she hoped to be among those chosen to begin a new Carmelite foundation in French Indochina (now North Vietnam), but her health was beginning to show signs of the tuberculosis that would claim her life. Even though she never left the Carmel of Lisieux during her brief life as a religious, her teaching and doctrine have spanned the world. In 1927, just thirty years after her death, she was proclaimed patroness of all missionaries and missions, a title she shares with Saint Francis Xavier.

This apostolic spirit influenced Saint Thérèse' spiritual discipline. She regularly prayed for others and had several "spiritual brothers," usually missionaries, for whom she was asked to pray in particular. Her attitude toward the Eucharist was similarly influenced; she recognized its intercessory potential and power. Thérèse rarely speaks of receiving Communion exclusively for her own benefit or intentions; ordinarily, her thoughts focus on one or several individuals whose need or predicament had been brought to her attention.

This practice was nurtured early in her life; even her First Communion was offered for someone else. She recalls:

> During the walks I took with Papa, he loved to have me bring alms to the poor we met on the way. On one occasion we met a poor man who was dragging himself along painfully on crutches. I went up to give him a coin. He looked at me with a sad smile and refused my offering since he felt he wasn't poor enough to accept alms. I cannot express the feeling that went through my heart.… I remembered having heard that on our First Communion Day we can obtain whatever we ask for, and this thought greatly consoled me. Although I was only six years old at the time, I said: "I'll pray for this poor man the day of my First Communion." I kept

my promise five years later, and I hope
God answered the prayer He inspired me
to direct to Him in favor of one of His
suffering members. (*Story*, II)

Throughout her life, Saint Thérèse expressed this
same generosity and compassion and concern, particularly as she formulated her intentions before
receiving Communion. On several occasions in her
correspondence she writes, "I will offer my Communion for you" (see *Letters*). Not surprisingly, the
last time she was physically able to receive Communion was offered for another person, an ex-priest
who had been a Carmelite.

By baptism we are incorporated into the Body
of Christ, we become part of a people committed
to following Jesus, proclaiming his message, and
promoting his mission. But often we live and work
in social contexts which insist upon the primacy
of the self as individualistic, independent, and even
isolated. The Eucharist, particularly its intercessory power, reminds us of our bonds with God and
with others. We are not created to be alone, we
are not designed to depend exclusively on our own
resources for everything. We need the other members
of the Body of Christ to assist, support, and en-

courage us, even as we bear the responsibility to assist, support, and encourage them.

The Eucharist is much more than a simple reminder of that truth, it celebrates and demonstrates that truth. Saint Thérèse challenges us to embrace fully our incorporation and participation in the Body of Christ as great privileges. We have access to the Lord and to many other followers of Jesus. The Eucharist unites us with them as with powerful and indispensable supports in our continuing efforts to pray for one another, to intercede for all those in need, and to transform our world.

"Everything is a grace"

Saint Thérèse often recalled important moments in her life by noting that they were times when she received Communion. Major feasts after her First Communion; during her trip to Rome in 1887 when she was bold enough to ask Pope Leo XIII personally if she could enter Carmel at an early age; her entrance into the monastery and other significant points during her religious life — the Eucharist is a part of all these events and led Thérèse to a deeper awareness of God's presence and activity within and around her. The Eucharist was a reference point for her, confirming that God was very much involved in her life, always and profoundly.

The Eucharist was a source of consolation for Thérèse, particularly when she could receive the sacrament frequently. During a very difficult time when many of the Sisters were ill and some were dying, she remembers, "All through the time the community was undergoing this trial, I had the unspeakable consolation of receiving Holy Communion every day" (*Story*, VIII). The consolation was never so much for her own satisfaction as it was a means of strengthening her resolve to please the Lord in all things. "I have offered myself to Jesus not as one desirous of her own consolation in His visit but simply to please Him who is giving Himself to me" (*ibid.*). Such is the challenge for all of us, to please the Lord whose self-gift to us is always accessible through the Eucharist.

As the tuberculosis ravaged Saint Thérèse' body, it became impossible for her to receive Communion and even to attend community prayer; the last time she received the sacrament was eight weeks before her death. It was a trial for her to be deprived of the Eucharist, especially in the midst of such a painful illness. On several occasions, her severe coughing and difficulty in breathing and swallowing prevented the successful completion of plans for her to receive Communion. Nevertheless, she was not discouraged: "Without a doubt, it's a great grace to receive the sacraments; but when God doesn't allow it, it's good just the same; everything is a grace" (*Last Conversations*, June 5).

For us, too, "everything is a grace" especially when seen with the conviction of God's love for us and through confidence in the Lord's transforming work within us. The Eucharist places ever before us the challenge of embracing God's love and welcoming that transformation. Thus, we can celebrate the Lord's longing to be always with us, knowing that we are loved. Saint Thérèse' teaching about the Eucharist is communicated to us primarily through the example of her life and her love relationship with the Lord. Through the Eucharist, she felt and knew that she was loved. In response, she dedicated her entire life to demonstrating and sharing that love with all people and in all situations. We are called to do the same. We are called, not only to receive the Eucharist, but to live it.

"In Remembrance of Me" —
This is Our Means For Mission

I received from the Lord what I also handed on to you, that the Lord Jesus on the night when he was betrayed took a loaf of bread, and when he had given thanks, he broke it and said, "This is my body that is for you. Do this in remembrance of me." In the same way he took the cup also, after supper, saying, "This cup is the new covenant in my blood. Do this, as often as you drink it, in remembrance of me." For as often as you eat this bread and drink the cup, you proclaim the Lord's death until he comes. (1 Corinthians 11:23-26)

Saint Paul handed on what he received; it became an intrinsic part of his preaching ministry among the people. From the very beginnings of Christianity, rooted in the example and teaching of Jesus, there was a developing awareness that the Eucharist, and the gospel itself, were not private possessions. By nature and purpose, they are meant to be shared and proclaimed. The Eucharist is a profound reminder of all that Jesus accomplished in his life, death, and resurrection; and it is a powerful message to be communicated. The Eucharist must be for us a means for mission.

The six spiritual guides who have led us through these reflections teach us those qualities that must configure our everyday life, tasks, and responsibilities. As we learn and live those qualities we become people of the Eucharist. The experiences through which God worked in the lives of these Doctors of the Church were uniquely their own; nevertheless, there is a weaving among those qualities of life to which they challenge and call us. Most of these saints lived and worked in distinct circumstances, at different historical periods. Still, there is a progression in the qualities they present that traces the basic lines of a rich Eucharistic spirituality; those lines mark the way for us to live and minister as people of the Eucharist.

Learning from Six Great Spiritual Guides

Our relationship with the Eucharist begins by God's loving initiative. Jesus comes among us, as one of us, and remains with us by his presence in the Eucharist, in the Church, and through the continuing work of the Holy Spirit. All this will remain little more than static historical data unless we choose to respond, unless we decide that the gift of Jesus' Eucharistic presence will make a significant difference in our life.

Saint Catherine of Siena teaches us that our response and decision are set in motion and sustained by our desire, our longing for God. This desire and longing assume that we recognize our need for God in life and our need for the nourishment provided by our participation in the Eucharist. If our recognition of those needs is not sufficiently sincere to urge us toward a response, then we do not move forward in our spiritual life because God's initiative will be met by an unresponsive heart. Saint Catherine reminds us that our response, indeed our life, must demonstrate our desire for God and our efforts to fulfill that desire through our relationship with Jesus in the Eucharist.

Through those efforts we gradually develop

an intimacy with the Lord which pervades every dimension and detail of our daily life. This intimacy is not meant to be the private reserve of only a few people. Saint Teresa of Avila insisted that intimacy with God was to be an identifying factor in the life of every Christian. This intimate relationship requires a growing familiarity founded upon frequent encounters with the Lord in the Eucharist and regular conversations in prayer. However intense and well developed it may become in time, our intimacy with the Lord is not self-sustaining. We are responsible for its vibrancy and vitality. Negligence of our spiritual life invites its gradual deterioration and, ultimately, its eventual diminishment altogether. By contrast, our relationship with the Lord will flourish through our fidelity to it.

Longing for God and intimacy with God are the solid groundwork upon which will be built our lasting union with God. Saint John of the Cross thoroughly explores that union and teaches us that this is primarily a union with the person and will of God. It is a process of divinization, of transformation into all that God has created us to be. This is the example that Jesus has established for us and that we are to follow. Therein is the wonder of the

Eucharist; it is a visible expression of the union with God to which Jesus calls us. Literally, Jesus becomes a part of us and dwells within us through the Eucharist. From Saint John's perspective, our primary task in the spiritual life is to be attentive to that union in every way possible and to detach ourselves from whatever could disrupt it. The gift of the Eucharist instructs and supports us in that attentiveness and detachment by demonstrating God's closeness to us and love for us. We need but live all that is unfolding within us through the Eucharist to affirm the transformation underway.

It is challenging and more than a bit daunting to consider the power inherent in the Eucharist and its potential for influencing our spiritual life. We may be tempted to hesitate in response to such an awesome gift, wondering if we are being called to live in a way that is far beyond our capacity. The wisdom of Saint Francis de Sales is particularly encouraging here. We do bear the responsibility to live all that our relationship with the Eucharist invites us to be. However, Saint Francis also teaches us that, by creation and with God's grace, we are capable of responding, we do have the capacity to live and love as Jesus lived and loved. The challenge of the Eucharist, then, is not so much a matter of whether we can be and do all that it calls us to be and do, but whether we will choose to respond to that call.

A Eucharistic spirituality and way of life are dynamic; they have a direction toward which they are moving. The end point of that dynamism and direction, of course, is nothing less than our transformation into the likeness of Jesus. Saint Alphonsus de Liguori affirms the accessibility of the Eucharist, thus reminding us of the proximity of our God. The ready access we have to Jesus in this sacrament is an encouragement and a support on our spiritual journey. Thus, once again, the question before us is not whether the Eucharist can facilitate our transformation but whether we will take full advantage of its accessibility to cooperate with and assent to that transformation.

On what basis can we be confident about all of this? What grounds do we have for believing that it is possible? Through the depth of her teaching and the eloquence of her example, Saint Thérèse of Lisieux points to the truth that makes all things possible: Jesus loves us and longs to be one with us. We should not underestimate the passion, power, and single-mindedness of Jesus' love and longing. It led him from the crib to the cross and beyond into new life. And his pursuit of us is not yet complete. Saint Thérèse emphasizes the truth of our lovability and the fact that Jesus seeks to find a home within us. Even when we acknowledge that truth, it can remain but a distant theory for us; we can yet struggle with seeing and accepting our value and worth in God's eyes and heart. Faith must be our guide here, for only in faith can our eyes and hearts be graced with God's perspective, only with faith can we embrace God's love for us.

Sketching a Eucharistic Spirituality

Some elements for a Eucharistic spirituality are evident in the teachings of these six Doctors of the Church; additional elements can be drawn from the vast store of wisdom within Church history and teaching, past and present. The four elements identified here constitute only a brief sketch, and yet they do reflect the riches of the Church's mystical tradition.

First, Eucharistic spirituality grounds itself in God's initiative on behalf of our salvation. Our response to that initiative is born of our desire for God. As we attend to that desire, we nurture and live an intimacy with God that gradually directs us toward union with God. Second, a Eucharistic way of life is not self-propelled. We must accept responsibility for the transforming union into which the Eucharist invites us. Admittedly, this is the work of God's grace, but that work neither counteracts nor diminishes our capacity for responding to grace. Third, Eucharistic spirituality affirms Jesus' love for us and his desire to establish a dwelling place within us. This affirmation can have a profound influence on our self-image and our understanding of human goodness. The extent of that influence will depend upon our openness to the workings of God's love within us. Fourth, a Eucharistic way of life is apostolic. It cannot be self-enclosed and still maintain a truly Eucharistic character. The transformation by love that takes place within us must reach beyond our individual lives to have a transforming impact on the world around us.

It is not surprising that Jesus gives us the gift of the Eucharist at the very beginning of the Paschal Mystery, prior to his passion and death. We need the support and sustenance that the Eucharist offers for what lies ahead — our encounters with the cross, our efforts in living the resurrection of Jesus, and our successes and failures in practicing the gifts of the Spirit in daily life. We celebrate the

Eucharist in remembrance of Jesus, not as a comforting act of nostalgia, but as an incentive to live Jesus' example and to proclaim the gospel in the midst of those encounters and efforts, successes and failures. Authentic remembrance is found in the actions that mark our everyday life, through all our activities and responsibilities.

In his encyclical *Ecclesia de Eucharistia* (On the Eucharist in Its Relationship to the Church), Pope John Paul II builds upon the teaching of the Second Vatican Council by referring to the Eucharist as "the source and the summit of all evangelization" (22). The Eucharist is both prayer and proclamation. Its transforming work within us is not meant to be self-contained. The effects of our relationship with the Eucharist must extend outward to our family and neighborhood, work environment and faith community, culture and country, Church and world. Then, through the example of our lives, we hand to others what Jesus has given to us.

"This is my body." "Do this is remembrance of me." This is our way of life. This is our means for mission. This is the source and summit of who we are and what we do as followers of Jesus. We thereby become people of the Eucharist.

Bibliography

Vatican Council II — The Conciliar and Post-Conciliar Documents, Volume 1; Austin Flannery, O.P., editor; New York: Costello Publishing Company, 1998.

Ecclesia de Eucharistia / On the Eucharist in Its Relationship to the Church, John Paul II; Boston: Pauline Books & Media, 2003.

Saint Catherine of Siena

Catherine of Siena — The Dialogue; Suzanne Noffke, O.P., translator; New York: Paulist Press, 1980.

The Prayers of Catherine of Siena; Suzanne Noffke, O.P., editor; New York: Paulist Press, 1983.

Saint Teresa of Avila

The Collected Works of St. Teresa of Avila; 3 volumes; Kieran Kavanaugh, O.C.D. and Otilio Rodriguez, O.C.D., translators; Washington, D.C.: ICS Publications, 1987.

The Letters of Saint Teresa of Jesus; 2 volumes; E. Allison Peers, translator; London: Sheed and Ward, 1980.

Saint John of the Cross

The Collected Works of St. John of the Cross; 3 volumes; Kieran Kavanaugh, O.C.D. and Otilio Rodriguez, O.C.D., translators; Washington, D.C.: ICS Publications, 1991.

Saint Francis de Sales

Francis de Sales, Jane de Chantal — Letters of Spiritual Direction; Péronne Marie Thibert, V.H.M., translator; New York: Paulist Press, 1988.

Introduction to the Devout Life; John K. Ryan, translator and editor; New York: Doubleday Bell Publishing Group, Inc., 1989.

The Love of God — A Treatise; Vincent Kerns, translator; Westminster: The Newman Press, 1962.

Saint Alphonsus de Liguori

Alphonsus de Liguori — Selected Writings; Frederick M. Jones, C.SS.R., editor; New York: Paulist Press, 1999.

Saint Thérèse of Lisieux

Saint Thérèse of Lisieux — General Correspondence; 2 volumes; John Clarke, O.C.D., translator; Washington, D.C.: ICS Publications, 1982.

Saint Thérèse of Lisieux — Her Last Conversations; John Clarke, O.C.D., translator; Washington, D.C.: ICS Publications, 1977.

Story of a Soul — The Autobiography of St. Thérèse of Lisieux; John Clarke, O.C.D., translator; Washington, D.C.: ICS Publications, 1996.

The Poetry of Saint Thérèse of Lisieux; Donald Kinney, O.C.D., translator; Washington, D.C.: ICS Publications, 1995.